The Enlightenment Teachings of Yogeshwar Muni

Self-Inquiry and Surrender Meditation in the Kripalu Yoga Tradition

Edited by

Richard Faulds

Peaceable Kingdom Books
Greenville, Virginia

Front and Back Cover: Photos of H. Charles Berner (Yogeshwar Muni) circa 1980 and 2002.

Copies of this book are available by mail. Send $15.00 (includes U.S. postage) to Danna Faulds, 53 Penny Lane, Greenville VA 24440

Wholesale price of $8.50 plus shipping available for purchases of five or more. For information, write yogapoems@aol.com

Printed in the U.S.A. by
Morris Publishing
3212 East Highway 30
Kearney, NE 68847
1-800-650-7888

This book is dedicated to

Yogeshwar Muni, an ardent practitioner and
dedicated teacher who departed this life June 24, 2007;

Lawrence Noyes, whose friendship made this book possible;

all the members of Yogeshwar Muni's spiritual communities
over the years who supported their teacher and called forth his
brilliance; and

those close disciples who were inspired by Yogeshwar's
example and have dedicated themselves to the practice of
Natural Yoga and continuing his legacy.

Also by Richard Faulds

Sayings of Swami Kripalu: Inspiring Quotes from a Contemporary Yoga Master (2004)

Kripalu Yoga: A Guide to Practice On and Off the Mat (Bantam 2005)

Swimming with Krishna: Teaching Stories from the Kripalu Yoga Tradition (2006)

Also by Danna Faulds

Go In and In: Poems From the Heart of Yoga (2002)

One Soul: More Poems From the Heart of Yoga (2003)

Prayers to the Infinite: Yoga Poems (2004)

From Root to Bloom, Poems and Other Writing (2006)

Limitless, Poems and Other Writing (2009)

All books except *Kripalu Yoga: A Guide to Practice On and Off the Mat* are available for $14 each or $8.50 each for purchases of five or more. For more information, contact Danna Faulds at yogapoems@aol.com or 53 Penny Lane Greenville VA 24440. We appreciate your support of us and Peaceable Kingdom Press.

4

The Lineage Lives

We are the energy of Shiva,
the vastness of the real,
the open space of silence
beyond mind. We are
timeless truth creating
itself anew.

The lineage lives in each
of us who choose to embody
its universal themes and
give shape and texture
to its dreams.

Danna Faulds

Table of Contents

Introduction

Yogeshwar Muni was a lineage holder in the Kripalu Yoga tradition who played a seminal role in the unique brand of American spirituality that burst upon the scene in the 1960s and continues to evolve today.

He was born Herman Charles Berner in 1929 in Colton, California. Encouraged to ask deep questions at an early age by his scientifically-minded parents, Berner embarked on the spiritual path while still a boy. His first enlightenment experience occurred while studying the *Tao Te Ching* as a teenager. By the age of twenty, Berner had commenced the teaching vocation he would continue until his death.

In the mid-1950s, Berner joined forces with the budding Scientology movement. The individuals attracted to Scientology and its founder, L. Ron Hubbard, in those early days were a pioneering group. Along with Berner, they included Werner Erhard, who went on to found EST, and Franklin Jones, who became the "crazy wisdom" teacher Da Free John.

Berner ran a Scientology field office in Costa Mesa and for a few years was President of the California church. Colleagues described his grasp of the mind clearing techniques upon which Scientology was founded as "unmatched." After all the scandals and bad press, it is tempting to ignore the fact that Scientology was a groundbreaking organization that influenced many individuals who later played prominent roles in the Human Potential Movement that emerged in the late 1960s.*

*Scientology was a religious organization established in 1952 to help people realize their deeper potential through a blend of science and the truths espoused in the Hindu, Buddhist, and Taoist scriptures.

7

In 1965, Berner began having serious doubts about the integrity of the Scientology organization. He objected to the command-and-control management imposed on teachers like himself and the coercive tactics used to market its services to the public. Disillusioned and ready to express his own vision of how people can grow and awaken, Berner cut his ties with Hubbard and the organization. He was targeted for retaliation, becoming one of the first defectors to suffer the harassment with which Scientology silenced its ex-members and critics.

Berner founded the Institute of Ability and formed a nonprofit organization to develop a rugged forty acre retreat center in the high desert east of Los Angeles. There he and his wife, Ava, explored holistic health techniques such as fasting and massage, communication exercises like those used in encounter groups, emotional release therapies, past life regression, and a host of other growth modalities popular among the 1960s counterculture. While most of his students were "hippies," it is noteworthy that Berner himself was not a product of the sixties and never saw drugs as a worthwhile way to raise consciousness.

Berner and Ava were impressed by the capacity of inter-personal communication to facilitate personal growth. They developed a set of communication techniques using "dyads," the name they gave to a pair of communicating partners. Struck by the power of these techniques to clear the mind, Berner began to question whether there was a more effective way for active-minded Westerners to pursue spiritual growth and self-realization than long hours of sitting meditation.

In a flash of inspiration, Berner had the idea to combine communication dyads with the "Who am I?" emphasis of Advaita Vedanta and the structured format of a Zen sesshin.

The result was the Enlightenment Intensive, a three-day retreat first offered in 1968. From the outset, the Enlightenment Intensive amazed Berner and participants with its ability to produce an authentic experience of "kensho" or temporary enlightenment.

Berner spent the next eight years leading Enlightenment Intensives and painstakingly refining its content and delivery. He developed a comprehensive protocol for training leaders, which was transcribed into a manual titled *The Transmission of Truth*. The teachings presented in the first half of this book are drawn from this manual and its later editions.* Enlightenment Intensives continue to be offered world wide. Search online for locations and more information.

In 1973, Berner's life was forever changed when he traveled to India and met Swami Kripalu. The headstrong Berner had known many yogis, mullahs, rinpoches and roshis, but he had never encountered a person of Swami Kripalu's caliber, someone to whom he was willing to submit and be guided by.

A revered monk no longer accepting students, Swami Kripalu saw something special in Berner too. He personally initiated Berner as one of a handful of direct disciples, giving him the name Yogeshwar Muni.

Berner came back to the States on fire to spread yoga. He publicly adopted the name Yogeshwar and moved to Berkeley, California, where he opened a yoga ashram to promulgate his distinctive interpretation of Swami Kripalu's teachings. While

*The updated manual *Consciousness of Truth* is available online at www.naturalmeditation.net. See also the less technical book *The Enlightenment Intensive: Dyad Communication as a Tool for Self-Realization* written by Lawrence Noyes in 1998.

many students fell away in his sudden transition to yoga guru, new ones took their place. Over the next five years, Swami Kripalu recognized Yogeshwar as his foremost Western disciple and bestowed on him the deepest teachings and empowerments of Shaktipat Kundalini Yoga.

Yogeshwar took steps to support his deepening yoga and meditation practice. He retired from giving Enlightenment Intensives in 1976, turning this part of his work over to able students. The nonprofit he ran bought a 110 acre canyon property in St. Helena, California, to establish a residential ashram and yoga retreat. The ashram community took root and gradually grew to over a hundred residents. Readers associated with Yogi Amrit Desai, an Indian-born disciple of Swami Kripalu, and his east coast Kripalu Center, may be surprised to learn they had a prominent American "uncle" and a cohort of California "cousins."*

In 1977, the reclusive Swami Kripalu stunned his Indian disciples by traveling to the United States. Intending to stay only four months, Swami Kripalu remained in the States the last four years of his life. While most of his time was spent at the Pennsylvania ashram of Yogi Desai, Swami Kripalu also visited Yogeshwar in California.

It was in St. Helena that Swami Kripalu delivered a masterful discourse entitled, "The Two Paths," answering Yogeshwar's plea for teachings to inspire both the monastic and householder members of his community. An excerpt of Swami Kripalu's

*Yogeshwar offered an Enlightenment Intensive at Desai's ashram in the mid-1970s that proved pivotal to Kripalu Center's future. Afterwards, Desai and his students adapted its basic format and dyad technique to create the Inner Quest Intensive and eventually a rich curriculum of yoga and personal growth programs.

discourse appears in Appendix A.

In the early 1980s, Yogeshwar began to feel the need for an isolated hermitage where he could focus exclusively on his spiritual practice. He also became convinced that the modern world economy was unstable and would inevitably collapse. Closing down his St. Helena ashram, Yogeshwar and a cadre of close disciples emigrated to Flaxley, South Australia, to establish a practice-based, permaculture community.

Yogeshwar's guiding vision for the community drew on the Hindu idea that the world unfolds in a predictable series of ages or *yugas*. He believed the destructive aspect of the current Kali Yuga had to flower fully before a new Golden Age could arise. This was to be a self-sufficient, seed community of yogis ready to sprout when the time was right.

While accepting of Yogeshwar's apocalyptic vision, most community members were there to live a wholesome back-to-the-land lifestyle, engage in spiritual practice, and benefit from their close association with a powerful teacher and spiritual guide. Although homesteading was hard work, the community grew to fifty members. It survived into the mid-1990s when, like Kripalu Center and so many other alternative communities, it suffered a painful breakup.

Yogeshwar left the community and abandoned his guru role to devote himself fully to his own spiritual practice. He settled in Merimbula, New South Wales, and was soon joined there by a small group of close students. Yogeshwar and the group gathered weekly to study scripture and support one another in their practices. This arrangement worked well for all concerned, and the teaching he did during these years flowed naturally. The spiritual progress made by Yogeshwar in his

11

later years was both apparent and inspiring to his students, and it was during this time that Yogeshwar produced some of his most important written works – see page 106.

I first learned of Yogeshwar Muni in the early 1980s during a volunteer stint at Kripalu Center. A close friend and yoga mentor, Yoganand Michael Carroll, gave me several photocopied binders of Swami Kripalu's unpublished writings. The teachings they contained became the foundation of my spiritual life, and I was grateful that Yogeshwar had paid an Indian scholar to translate them from Gujarati into English.

While a Kripalu ashram resident in the late 1980s, I happened upon a spiral bound booklet written by Yogeshwar titled *Natural Meditation.* * The method of surrender it espoused intrigued me, and I read it straight through several times. As the content gradually seeped into my practice, I realized that Yogeshwar was more than a student of Swami Kripalu. He was a potent teacher in his own right. The teachings presented in the second half of this book come primarily from this booklet, which was revised by Yogeshwar in 2004.

It wasn't until 1999 that Yogeshwar's genius came clear to me. It was then that I took my first Enlightenment Intensive. Over the course of three demanding days, Yogeshwar's contemplation technique enabled me to break through barriers that had proved impervious to the healing and growth-oriented approach of Kripalu Yoga.

Natural Meditation is the original name Yogeshwar used for the surrender method featured in this book. Later he switched to *Natural Yoga* because meditation does not accurately describe the whole process that ensues after surrender. This book uses Natural Meditation to avoid confusion with other teachers and traditions referring to their approaches as Natural Yoga.

Looking back, it's clear that I desperately needed Yogeshwar's uncompromising stance and intellectual rigor to cast light on the true nature of self. After years of drying the wood through Desai's heartfelt and feeling-based teachings, it was the Enlightenment Intensive that sparked the blaze I'd been seeking.

Afterward, I vowed to learn everything there was to know about Enlightenment Intensives. My first step was to seek out Lawrence Noyes in Toronto, where I trained to lead Intensives myself. The ten day course gave me an opportunity to study the Enlightenment Intensive manuals, go through the training protocols, and get to know a lifelong friend.

Lawrence had been a close student of Yogeshwar and leading member of the California and South Australia ashram communities. He opened his heart to me, and later shared his personal archive of ashram publications. Without Lawrence, this book would not be in your hands.

This book is not a simple restatement of Yogeshwar's written works. It's my attempt to distill his views into a user-friendly primer that brings a solid set of enlightenment teachings to Kripalu Yoga practitioners.

While enlightenment work is just one facet of human development, it's one obscured by many myths and mistaken notions. Perhaps the most damaging of these is that enlightenment is something to be pursued at the end of the spiritual path – versus the beginning.

In this context, Natural Meditation is a post-enlightenment practice that incorporates hatha and raja yoga to stabilize and deepen your enlightenment.

In working with the materials upon which this book is based, I endeavored to present Yogeshwar's teachings simply and in his own words. A pragmatic teacher, Yogeshwar's best medium of communication was informal talks delivered to groups of students. I resisted the desire to overly polish the transcripts of these talks in order to preserve the power of his spoken voice.

While every effort was made to remain true to the original sources, the text has been edited and paraphrased as necessary to make it succinct and accessible. In places, I combined materials from different places to convey a whole message on a particular topic. Because this type of editing by necessity entails interpretation, I'd like readers to know that an online library of Yogeshwar's works can be found at www.naturalmeditation.net.

Yogeshwar Muni died on June 24, 2007, surrounded by loving students. I am deeply grateful for the legacy of teachings and techniques he left behind. From here on out, the voice behind the words is Yogeshwar's. Blessings to his soul – and yours.

Richard Faulds
Greenville, Virginia

Who You Are

Who you are is so much more
than what you do. The essence,
shining through heart, soul, and
center, the bare and bold truth
of you does not lie in your
to-do list. You are not just
at the surface of your skin, not
just the impulse to arrange the
muscles of your face into a smile
or a frown, not just boundless
energy, or bone wearying fatigue.
Delve deeper. You are divinity;
the vast and open sky of Spirit.
It's the light of God, the ember
at your core, the passion and the
presence, the timeless, deathless
essence of you that reaches out
and touches me. Who you are
transcends fear and turns
suffering into liberation.
Who you are is love.

Danna Faulds

Chapter One
What Enlightenment Is Not

I want to share with you everything I know about getting enlightened. When I discuss these things with students, I normally don't bother to explain much. I just say, "do this and don't do that." Here, I want to give you the reasons, and describe some of my experiences, so you won't have to learn everything the hard way.

On the path to enlightenment, you will undoubtedly come up against some barriers. Whether what's blocking you is physical, emotional or mental, my job is to help you get through what you don't think you can get through. I won't spend a lot of time convincing you why pursuing enlightenment is a good idea. Everyone who's ever broken through to the enlightened state says it was worth the effort. I'll assume you can do it. Even if you can't, I'll assume that you're going to do it anyway, and we'll just bust through.

One big problem is that enlightenment can't be expressed in words. The best any teacher can do is point in the right general direction, and that's what I'm going to do here.

I've found the right place to start is saying what enlightenment is not. Enlightenment is not a verbal definition. It's helpful to have clear-cut definitions of what words mean, and to tag the right words onto an idea. If a teacher asks you, "What is life?," you might respond "Life is a growing process." No matter how satisfied you are with your answer, that kind of understanding is not enlightenment.

Enlightenment is also not the same as insight. An insight is an internal seeing that occurs through a mental process of perception, reflection, reasoning, and intuition. Suddenly, you see something that you have never seen before. Afterward, you might say, "Ahhh, I feel it. I know it. It's true." Insights are powerful and beneficial, one of the greatest thrills you can have in life. But they are not enlightenment.

The difference between enlightenment and insight is that an insight occurs through a mental process. Enlightenment is a direct knowing that is process-less. Any process that you have been going through stalls as you near the onset of enlightenment. Many people in the therapeutic community equate insight with enlightenment. This is a degradation of the word "enlightenment" and the spiritual traditions based upon it.

Sometimes there are all kinds of flashy side effects that precede, accompany, or follow an enlightenment experience. These are not enlightenment either. I call these side effects "phenomena." You may find your body coursing with energy, shaking with chills, or rolling around on the floor. You might feel terrified that you are going to die or go insane. You may fall into comforting states of bliss, gain profound insight, or see light emanating out of you. How many aspirants have been sidetracked by these fascinating distractions?

In truth, most people are not striving for enlightenment; they are just trying to get some sort of powerful experience. Whether it's enlightenment or not doesn't really matter to them. They innocently accept white lights, visions, or intense emotional and energy experiences as enlightenment because they don't know any better.

After I had given fifteen Enlightenment Intensives, I decided to take one led by a person I'd trained. I was going great guns when out of a spot of light came hundreds of beautiful

17

butterflies. They just poured out, luscious five-colored butterflies, and I was tempted to sit there and watch them. Knowing better, I resisted the temptation. The butterflies kept coming out of the spot of light, but I just went on with my contemplation. Fifteen minutes later, I had a deep enlightenment experience.

It's not always like that. Sometimes enlightenment occurs without any phenomena worth mentioning. The side effect is like a soft breath of air, just a puff, accompanied by a thought like, "How could I have missed anything so obvious?"

Any enlightenment experience can be divided into two parts: the fact and the phenomena. The fact is a fundamental change in consciousness. You are conscious one way, and then you are conscious in another way. The phenomena is anything that happens to go along with it. Unfortunately the phenomena starts to come on before the fact, and if you get distracted you won't make it through.

While phenomena may be a symptom that you are drawing near the gap that separates the unenlightened and enlightened states, don't be seduced into thinking that phenomena are enlightenment. They are not enlightenment.

Phenomena can be compared to someone walking down a hallway and kicking something out of the way to get to the other end. Whatever is blocking your entry into the enlightened state is producing the phenomena. Does it really matter what needs to get kicked out of the way?

Getting enlightened is not easy, but just because something is not easy is no reason to sell it down the river. It's a major error to accept definitions, insights, emotional excitement, or phenomena as enlightenment. If you come to me and say, "Oh Yogeshwar, I had this experience of the great shimmering shimmeringness of all shimmeringness and now I'm enlightened," expect me to nod encouragingly and send you back to your contemplation. Don't succumb to surrogates when the Truth itself lies just beyond your fingertips.

Chapter Two
Enlightenment Defined

When it comes to defining enlightenment, teachers fall into two schools of thought. Buddha is the best example of the first school. He didn't say much of anything about the enlightened state. In fact, he refused to discuss the subject directly.

Lao Tsu and Meher Baba are good examples of the second school. Lao Tsu wrote the *Tao Te Ching*, a masterful description of impersonal enlightenment. There is a book by Meher Baba called *God Speaks*. A lot of people thought Meher Baba was crazy. A lot of people thought he was God. I respect him as a masterful metaphysician, and if you can get through his book you will find a first-class description of enlightenment from the personal perspective.

Teachers like Buddha know that enlightenment is not an idea of any sort, correct or otherwise. They've seen how students can trick themselves into believing they're enlightened simply because they intellectually grasp some definition of it. Having passed through the barriers to enlightenment, these teachers know that all concepts must be set aside in order to directly experience truth. So they choose not to add their ideas to the pile their students have already acquired.

After many years, I have come down on the other side, concluding that it's better to *correctly* define enlightenment. You probably believe to some extent what our culture has told you about who and what you are. To make matters worse, you are living your life guided by these deep seated and erroneous ideas. Seeing what you are up against, it's a shallow approach to not define enlightenment, even if it is one more preconception that you have to work through. I've seen a clear definition tip the scale for people, inspiring them to set mistaken notions aside and turn their attention toward a correct idea, making the truth itself only one small step away.

With all that said, you'll have to forgive me because I'm not going to pull any punches. What I'm about to give you is the result of my experience over thirty years of spiritual endeavor.

Enlightenment is a conscious state of direct knowledge of yourself as you truly are.* That's a big thought to get straight in your head, but the crux of it lies in just a few phrases: *conscious state*; *direct knowledge*; and *yourself as you truly are*. Let's go through each of these with a fine toothed comb.

You already know what it means to be in a conscious state. You have a field of conscious awareness and its content is constantly changing. If you are aware of the impressions, thoughts, feelings, memories, images, and other things in that field, then you are in a conscious state.

Have you ever been so drunk that you woke up the next day and found yourself in bed with your car parked sideways on the porch and no memory of how it all happened? Now, during that time you were still you, but you weren't noticing yourself – you weren't in a conscious state.

---

*In his 1977 manual, Yogeshwar described enlightenment as "direct experience," a term intimately coupled with the questions he taught to pursue enlightenment, chief among them, "Tell me who you are" and "Tell me what you are." The result was a description of enlightenment as the direct experience of the truth of who you are, or what you are. In the 2006 revision of the manual, *Consciousness of Truth*, Yogeshwar defined enlightenment as stated above.

Some people sleepwalk their way through life, stimulus-response mechanisms with hardly any reflective consciousness. You have to begin wherever you find yourself, and for many that means raising your awareness of what you're thinking and feeling, and being willing to acknowledge how things really are for you.

There are all sorts of elevated states of consciousness, and some people spend a lot of time and effort getting into them, but that's not what I am talking about here. Being in a conscious state just means that you are awake and aware.

Direct knowledge may be a new idea to you. When you think of how you know something, you usually think of indirect knowledge: consciously receiving information through your senses and processing it with your brain. This is the way you know things in everyday life, and it works well enough for that purpose. It's indirect because it happens through a process.

You look at a wall, and there is the perceptual process of seeing. Light bounces off the wall and strikes the retina. Nerve cells in the retina feed information to the brain. The nerve signals get passed around to four or five brain centers and end up as a visual image of a wall. You are not directly experiencing the wall; you are perceiving it indirectly through the process of seeing. The reason I am making this distinction is because directness is the critical factor in enlightenment.

So what exactly do I mean by the word *direct*? There is no special, sneaky, esoteric definition. It means just what it means in the English language. I can hint around the edges, but in the end you need to be satisfied with a primitive notion. Direct knowledge means knowing through no means or process, with nothing interposed in between.

You could get off track here by thinking I'm using the words *direct knowledge* to describe the process of feeling. Feeling is a little more direct way of knowing than mental processes, but it isn't going to get you enlightened. It's only by removing any process that you have a chance at enlightenment.

You've got to get over all sensing, feeling, thinking, reasoning, trying, struggling, hoping, believing, analyzing, remembering, concluding, and even seeing with your mind's eye. Now you're probably frustrated and want to say, "So exactly how am I supposed to have this direct experience?" That's the whole point; there's no "how" involved.

Direct knowledge can be described as *just knowing*, like the way you know anything that requires no thought process – your name for instance, or how to ride a bicycle, or where the kitchen is in your house.

Direct knowledge of yourself differs from these examples in one important way. Each of them is based on a prior history of learning. Your ability to know yourself is intrinsic, a fundamental and timeless ability of every individual. With enlightenment, there is no sense of *Now I know what I didn't know before.* It is, *I've always known; I just didn't know that I knew.*"

Right now you may believe that you are a body, or a brain, or a personality, or a soul, or a spirit, or a hundred other things. Many people who are pretty spiritually advanced think of themselves as consciousness.* In truth, you are none of these things. The mystery of what you actually are can only be solved by illuminating it, i.e. by becoming conscious of your true nature. To do that, you have to disentangle yourself from all these false identifications.

With enlightenment, you know yourself as you truly are, directly and without any process of reasoning or remembering. You are not a soul. You are not a spirit. Such concepts are nonsense. Yet they do point to something true, something immaterial and unlimited that can be known through your own direct experience.

In the absolute immediacy of enlightenment, you become conscious of yourself as you truly are – a nonphysical entity with the power of free will and choice, uncaused, ageless, existing outside of time, with no location in space. Enlightenment reveals the existence of what I call the *true individual*.

While a correct definition of enlightenment can point you in the right direction, an authentic enlightenment experience of this true individual completely dispels the illusion of physicalness. You already are the transcendent; you're just masking it through ignorance.

I was taking an Enlightenment Intensive some years back and had this raging fever. My head was burning up, and I felt like I was spinning and ready to pass out. Somehow I was able to

---

* Curiously, direct knowledge itself is not conscious. It happens in the dark and silence of the preconscious. However, when you know yourself directly, you also become conscious of your true nature. This is enlightenment. For more, see the 2006 manual online.

hold on in the face of that phenomena. By whatever grace there may be, this brilliant light came from the infinite resources of the universe. Then that light, more brilliant than ten million suns, ceased to be a perception, and I was just conscious of the Absolute, and it was both personal and impersonal.

Up until that experience, I called it Truth. Because of my scientific training, that was the orientation I'd taken. After that experience, I called it God. It ceased being a concept and became a living thing for me, something I'm aware of constantly and under all circumstances. Even if I am yelling at you, and you are yelling at me, that experience is never lost.

The light was not the truth. The light was just a harbinger. For most of my life, I had read about this sort of thing and thought, "Well, maybe it's true," but in spite of my efforts I had always failed. So I began to think that maybe all these religious figures were just spouting fantasy, or trying to sell people a bill of goods. Now I know otherwise.

There are not different kinds of enlightenment. There is not one enlightenment you get in Buddhism, another from Yoga, and another from Christianity.* Yes, there are different depths and magnitudes of enlightenment. We'll discuss that later, but there is only one kind of enlightenment and that is conscious, direct knowledge of yourself as you truly are.

*Yogeshwar's point that enlightenment can only come from self-knowledge is mirrored in the Gospel of Thomas, wherein Jesus instructs Thomas: "Examine yourself and learn who you are. Although you do not understand it yet, you will be called 'the one who knows himself.' For whoever has not known himself knows nothing, but whoever has known himself has simultaneously come to know the depth of all things."

25

Chapter Three
The Value of Enlightenment

You might wonder why anyone would want to do what it takes to get enlightened. The primary value of enlightenment is intrinsic – it's enlightenment itself. No matter how brief the experience, enlightenment fulfills your purpose in life, which is to know the truth of who and what you are.

Enlightenment also has a secondary benefit; it can be applied to your life. People evolve through three basic phases of human development. The first is childhood's age of innocence, where you are dependent and fairly helpless. In the second phase, you learn how to exert your will, live by rules, and gain self-discipline. You get your act together – or at least try to – in order to live a successful life.

In this phase, you can get by thinking of yourself as a body, a mind-based personality, or one of many social masks and false identities. It won't be very satisfying, but you can pass muster with this kind of confused idea of yourself. This is where most of the world's people are today.

The doorway to the third phase is self-discovery, which gives you the capacity to live your life from who you truly are. You can now achieve a level of effectiveness and fulfillment that was unavailable to you before. You cease going through the motions and learn that your life does not have to be shallow and dull. You can make real progress toward real goals, and be truly happy, because it is now you living your life rather than some personality or false self with which you have wrongly identified. The key to making the shift into this third phase is gaining conscious, direct knowledge of who you are.

I had been teaching spiritual growth techniques for some years when I noticed something important. The progress of those students who thought they were bodies or minds was agonizingly slow. Instead of them doing the growth technique, it was done through the medium of whatever self-concept they had unwittingly become identified with. Even if the growth technique worked and brought about a desired change in awareness, it wouldn't really impact their ability to choose and act differently.

So I invented a little exercise in which I would have people notice that they had a body and mind. I'd have them touch their flesh, feeling it with their hands, and I'd say, "That's the body." Then I'd have them imagine a cat they've known, visualize themselves stroking its back and hearing it purr, and I would say, "That cat is part of the mind." Then I'd complete the exercise by instructing them, "Now notice who is looking at the cat."

Many people in many disciplines have made this distinction between the individual and the mind. Often they call it the *seat of consciousness*, which implies the individual is the center of consciousness While on the right track, they haven't finished the job in my opinion. The true individual is not consciousness; it is the one capable of consciousness. You could say that a human being is a combination of a body, a brain, a mind, a personality, and the actual individual. Here I am talking about the individual.* If you can understand this distinction, you can understand enlightenment.

*This true individual is the one you aim to directly experience in enlightenment work. The Cat Exercise is a "self-discovery" technique that produces a shallow experience that is qualitatively different from enlightenment.

In working with students, I found that pointing out who you are in the Cat Exercise was not sufficient by itself, so I developed other techniques to help people directly experience who and what they are. Some of these have proved effective at reaching great depths of enlightenment. That said, there is still a valuable seed experience in the Cat Exercise.

Knowing who you are, the true individual who has free will, and knowing who you are not, the programmed mind and personality, is a real step forward. It enables you to take any growth technique and apply it to make rapid progress. It transports you from the concept-land of reading, thinking, and talking about spiritual growth to the reality of living from a conscious, direct experience of yourself as you truly are.

In the end there's no easy path to enlightenment. You can go straight up the cliff, or climb slowly and carefully, but either way you are going to sweat and bang up your shins. The thing to remember is that everyone who's ever made the trip says the effort was worth it.

Chapter Four
The Enlightenment Technique

It seemed to me that the age old technique of contemplating the question "Who am I?" was a very good one. Unfortunately, it's not easy to do. If it was, you'd get enlightened on the first shot. The problem is the mind, which is chock full of things that are pending or not fully understood.

Did you ever have a desk with a box marked "pending" on it? That's a lot like the mind. Something comes in the box and you say, "I'm going to get right on it." While you are handling this task, ten more come in. You can't do them all at one time, so you glance at the top sheet and decide, "I don't really understand this one; I'll work on it later." So you go on to something else, and in the meantime the task you set aside gets stored in the mind.

You have a similar outgoing box in which you send messages to others. Some of them never get picked up or delivered. These un-received messages also get stored in the mind. Along with them are past experiences that were too intense for you to digest. These get stowed away for future integration. Then there are all sorts of ideas and problems that you acquired from your social environment that you have not been able to understand or resolve. The list goes on and on.

When you go to contemplate "Who am I?," the mind begins to throw up all these stored ideas, memories, fears, traumatic experiences, suppressed feelings, false identifications, and confusions that are somehow related to your sense of self. This is why it can take years and years of solo meditation to find your way through the morass of the mind.

Rather than thrashing about in the quicksand of thought-land, I developed a dyad technique to keep you focused on your contemplation despite all the mind's machinations. It is based on two specific instructions: "Tell me who you are" and "Tell me what you are."*

Contemplation techniques always utilize an object of contemplation, like a scriptural verse or religious icon. In this case, it's you – the actuality of who or what you are. Since enlightenment is direct knowledge of yourself, it would be inefficient or even misleading to pursue it through any other object of contemplation.

After receiving the instruction from you partner, contemplation begins with *intending to directly experience* who or what you are. To do this, you've got to understand what intent means. In plain English, it means you are going to do something. If you intend to go to Hong Kong, there's more involved than hoping, wishing, or trying. You are not sitting there musing, "Maybe someday I will visit Hong Kong; maybe I won't."

You are not daydreaming about Hong Kong and what it might be like to be there. Intent has a commitment in it. If you were to say, "I am going to Hong Kong," that is intent. In this technique, you would say, "I am going to directly experience myself as I truly am." You mean it, and you are going to do it.

We've already talked about the word direct; it means without any process or means, without any "how." You are not trying

*These teachings were designed for the Enlightenment Intensive, which utilizes a contemplation and communication technique done with a partner – see page 35 for a detailed description. In this chapter, the text stays true to Yogeshwar's original dyad technique, with footnotes describing how to adapt it for solo contemplation.

to figure out who you are, you are not trying to formulate a correct answer to your question, you are intending to directly experience yourself as you truly are.

The next step in the technique is to be open to whatever may occur in your consciousness as a result of your intention. You know what open means. If you open a door, the door is open. If you open a can of beer, the can is open.

In this case, it means to leave your field of consciousness open to whatever may occur as a result of your contemplation. As I explained, you have all sorts of preconceived ideas about who you are and what enlightenment is like. These are stowed away in your mind. Let go of all your preconceived ideas, and just be open to whatever may occur.

Two different kinds of events are likely to occur in your field of awareness. The first are things that are not the result of your intention to directly experience yourself. These are to be ignored. Maybe you are tired of sitting up and your back is hurting. Okay, good to know, but you can ignore this because you don't see any connection between that and your contemplation.

You should not try to wrestle with this kind of occurrence; you should not try to clear them out of the mind; you should not look them over and investigate them. They are distractions, and ignoring them is a very powerful technique. When you don't add your life energy to something, it tends to wither.

Events will also occur in your field of awareness as a result of your intention to directly experience yourself. These get communicated to your partner, without adding anything or leaving anything out.

Don't skip over something just because it seems obvious. Don't be judgmental and censor anything that you feel won't be acceptable or understood by others. Just say whatever it is in a way that gets it across to your partner. When you've said it, a piece of paper in your in-basket has been read, and you can throw it away.*

At this point, you return to where you began and cycle through the technique again:

1. Come back to your question: who or what are you?
2. Intend to directly experience yourself as you truly are.
3. Remain open to whatever arises in your field of awareness as a result of your contemplation.
4. Communicate that to your partner.**

As a general rule, you should spend roughly equal amounts of time contemplating and communicating. Some people tend to spend all their time contemplating. Others spend all their time communicating. These are both technique errors that will

*This is where the teachings of Kripalu Yoga dovetail beautifully to provide a solo form of contemplation. Instead of communicating to a partner, a solo contemplator practices deep inner listening. Notice whatever occurs in your field of awareness as a result of your contemplation. See it clearly by witnessing with compassion. Feel it fully by riding any associated waves of sensation or emotion. Choose to be present to your experience, neither making anything happen, nor keeping anything that wants to naturally happen from flowing to completion. These core Kripalu Yoga techniques enable a solo contemplator to be his or her own listening partner. This is not meant to imply that solo contemplation replaces or produces the same experience as the Enlightenment Intensive.

** Or process it internally if practicing solo contemplation.

impede your progress. Divide your time about evenly between contemplation and communication.*

Doing this technique will probably not give you a direct experience right away. It will give you a lot of indirect experiences. As these indirect experiences keep happening, they tend to empty out the mind and feelings. Persisting, you will dissolve away the things that come into the forefront of your mind as a result of your contemplation.

You are not trying to dissolve the entire mind, which is a big undertaking. You are taking one part of the mind, the part related to who you are, and working there until the pile on your desk is gone. Eventually, that part of your mind will be clear and you'll have what might be called a blank mind.

Many people confuse having a blank mind with enlightenment. It is not enlightenment, and if someone tells you otherwise they are simply wrong. Clearing the mind sets up a situation in which enlightenment is likely to occur. You can now do the technique, intending to directly experience who you truly are, without the mind interposing its ideas, memories, conclusions, beliefs, traumas, and other things into your field of consciousness. When the mind is gone and the only thing left is you contemplating the truth of you, the probability of having an enlightenment experience is considerably enhanced.

*The intention to directly experience yourself as you truly are is like a sharp knife that slices through any layers of misidentification separating you from self-knowledge. Openness and noticing what arises allow the severed layer to fall away. In solo contemplation, these processes braid together as contemplation deepens, but both strands of active contemplation and deep inner listening should remain.

Unfortunately, I've seen people sit in this state for hours and still not directly experience the truth of their existence. What can be done about that? Beyond sticking with the technique and ignoring the phenomena that are likely to occur, there is almost nothing that can be done.

Somewhere along the line, you will either directly experience who you are, or you won't. In the end, enlightenment is not a willful thing. It's a spontaneous event, a grace of sorts that you cannot make happen. All you can do is set up a situation in which the probability is maximized. The contemplation technique I have just given you is designed to do just that, and it works.*

*The communication aspect of the Enlightenment Intensive is what distinguishes it from solo contemplation. Yogeshwar believed that it was the reception of a contemplator's communication by a listening partner, and the resulting experience of being understood by another person, that enabled the mind to be cleared so quickly.

The Enlightenment Technique

1.   Dyad Position: Two individuals sitting at a comfortable distance. By virtue of their position in the room, one assumes the role of the listening partner, and the other the contemplating partner.

2.   Giving the Instruction: The listening partner instructs the contemplating partner to *"Tell me who you are"* or *"Tell me what you are."*

3.   Receiving the Instruction: The contemplating partner accepts the instruction as a sincere request from the listening partner for communication.

4.   Contemplation Process: the contemplating partner begins a contemplation process that includes the following three steps:

- **Contact the Actuality.** A woman working on the question *Who am I?* gets a sense of who she is, in the moment, as best she can.

- **Intend to Directly Experience It.** After contacting the actuality, she intends to experience it directly. The intention to directly experience is different than thinking about or reflecting upon. It is intending to experience the thing itself without the filter of feelings, concepts or thoughts.

- **Remain Open.** While holding this intention, she remains open to a direct experience of self, and to whatever occurs in her body, emotions, or mind as a result of this intention. Remaining open means to leave awareness free of preconceived ideas about what your experience should be and not try to make anything happen.

5. Communication: The contemplating partner then communicates to the listening partner whatever occurred as a result of her contemplation, not adding anything or leaving anything out. This is different than free association, in which anything that arises in the body or mind is communicated. Only those things that occur as a result of contemplation are communicated. Other things are ignored. Communication is more than just saying it out loud. An attempt is made to get it across to the listening partner.

6. A Balance of Contemplation and Communication: The contemplator repeats the process of contemplating and communicating, keeping a rough balance of time spent in each, until five minutes have elapsed and a gong sounds.

7. Listening: The listening partner watches, listens and tries to understand, without commenting, giving social cues like nodding, or evaluating in any way.

8. Acknowledgment: When the gong sounds, the listening partner says *thank you*, acknowledging that the communication was received.

9. Change Over: Partners switch roles and repeat the above process four times each, taking a total of 40 minutes.

10. Structured Schedule: The Enlightenment Technique is repeated for three days, starting at 6:00 AM and running through 11:00 PM, amidst a supportive schedule of light meals, walking contemplation, instructional talks, rest and exercise periods, and other activities.

Chapter Five
Identification and De-Identification

To understand how the contemplation technique works, and what takes place when enlightenment occurs, you need to understand identification. The crux is simple: identification occurs when the true individual mistakenly identifies with something it is not. Enlightenment is conscious, direct knowledge of yourself as you truly are, which can only occur when all false identification has ceased.

Identification occurs innocently. You were born and got to the diaper stage. One day you found yourself running around the front yard playing in the sprinkler and thinking of yourself as this little body. You didn't say to yourself, "I am going to forget what I really am." It doesn't happen like that. You innocently and unconsciously begin to think of yourself as the body because of the constant barrage of information you received from the senses.

All identification takes place in a similar fashion. You identify with the body, senses, mind, emotions, and a personality that contains a whole attitude and approach to life. You engage in the activities of life thinking: "I am the seer; I am the hearer; I am the feeler; I am the desirer; I am the doer; I am the one who experiences all these things." You see everything through the lens of your perceptual viewpoint and personality, which colors your interpretation of your life experience.

Let's assume you have a deep-seated attitude that you are inadequate. Even if you do something that is pretty good, your personality will still interpret it as inadequate. "I always screw things up." Or you may believe you are glorious and interpret something not very good as, "Oh, what a fantastic thing I did."

37

Neither of these interpretations is correct; both have been distorted by the lens of your personality.

Once I was leading an Enlightenment Intensive and a participant was asked, "Tell me who you are." His response was to pull out his driver's license and show it to his partner. This was his identity.

Along with personal information like your name, date of birth, and family of origin, you also identify with all sorts of ideas in your mind, personality traits you've adopted, states of being to which you've grown accustomed, social masks you project, and reputations you defend. You are like an actor who has forgotten that you are playing a role.

All of this material with which you've identified is stored in the mind and interferes with your contemplation. In doing the technique, the mind and personality are always between you and the object you aspire to consciously, directly know – yourself as you truly are. The intention to directly experience your self gradually erodes away the layers of identification underlying your personality. This process of "de-identification" is a real project, because you are only dimly aware of all the beliefs, material things, and states of being you are identified with.

In the early stages of contemplation, a lot of peripheral thoughts and experiences come into the field of your awareness. You won't get your deep-seated attitudes of inadequacy or gloriousness right away. What comes up first are all these distorted memories of experiences that were colored by your attitudes. You will see and feel how it was for you to move through life with a fixed attitude of inadequacy or gloriousness.

Most people give up at this point because they grow frustrated at not coming up with anything that feels like progress. They are defeated by the mind. If you persist with the technique, you will get through all the layers of superficial identification and erroneous thinking of yourself as this or that. You will also get through the deeper layers of identification with the body, mind, and personality that are the major barriers to enlightenment.

This process of discerning "what you are not" reflects real progress. You are likely to become blank-minded after that and find yourself peering out into space, trying to see what you are. If you persistent at this, you are likely to exhaust yourself and start to hallucinate.

The truth is that you are not a looker, desirer, doer, or experiencer. You are still identified with these basic points of view. If you can disentangle yourself from these, you are likely to still be identified with consciousness. If you arrive here, you have made a lot of progress, going all the way from thinking of yourself as your driver's license to mistaking yourself as consciousness.

Yet you are still short of the absolute truth of yourself. Yes, there is consciousness, but the true individual is not consciousness. You are the one who is capable of consciousness. Do you see how subtle things get?

Because consciousness has no materiality to it, you may find yourself conceiving of yourself as an empty nothing. What you are missing in all these blank mind states is the intention to have conscious, direct knowledge of what you are, right where you are. Instead of looking out and trying to see, feel or sense yourself, you must catch yourself right where you are.

The moment of de-identification feels like death. When you cease to be something you were convinced you were, there is a moment of complete annihilation of consciousness before the next identification arises. Whether shifting states or having an enlightenment experience, there is always this discontinuity, this break in consciousness.

It's common to want to turn and run at this point. You don't want to bring about the death of that which you are accustomed to thinking of yourself as being. Yet the process is not dangerous. You go through the same barrier every time you go to sleep and wake up. If I were to reassure you that you did the same thing just this morning, you might reply, "I didn't do that; it just happened by itself." Then I would add, "That's the way this is going to happen too, but you have to be open to it."

De-identification does not guarantee enlightenment. It just makes it possible. Enlightenment always occurs through what could be called grace, a leap of faith, or good fortune. But at the moment of de-identification from any state of being, a crack opens in the psyche and there is a possibility of enlightenment.*

I've seen how some people are able to notice the moment of de-identification. This gives them conscious, direct knowledge of the true individual that just de-identified from whatever it was identified with a moment earlier. These people get enlightened quickly. Others continue to look out, expecting to get something other than themselves. They think, "I don't want me. I already have that."

*While the contemplation technique empties out the mind and raises the likelihood of enlightenment, it's important to know that people de-identify and have enlightened experiences at any time during an Enlightenment Intensive and not just when they have a blank mind.

There's a beautiful story about a Japanese man seeking enlightenment. He got on his horse and galloped all over the countryside, looking here and there, until he finally came upon a Zen master.

The man got off his horse, walked up to the master, and said, "I want to become enlightened. I've been looking everywhere." The master said, "Why aren't you looking for a horse?"

The man was perplexed and said, "I already have a horse." The Zen master smiled and walked away.

If you persist with the technique, that's what it comes down to. When you are looking for enlightenment, you are the one you are looking for. That is why some people laugh hysterically when they get enlightened. Nothing is more obvious than the truth of your own existence, but all the stuff in the mind, all the innocent identifications, and the preconceived notion that you are going to discover something other than yourself, stop you from noticing it.

In a way, enlightenment is a total rip off, because you don't get anything you don't already have. Yet it's worth everything to have the issue of who you are settled once and for all.

Chapter Six
Facing a Crisis

If enlightenment was easy, anyone with a sincere interest would already be enlightened. The difficulty comes from the barriers and crises you encounter along the way.

Say you are on a journey and come up against a little hillside. Some effort is required, but you know you can walk over it, so it's not a crisis. But say you come across a 29,000 foot mountain peak and scramble your way up to 28,000 feet. A blizzard blows in and you don't feel you can make it. Now you've got a crisis on your hands.

If you are doing the technique, you are going to confront crises. Aspirants have sought enlightenment for thousands of years. They dedicated their whole lives to the pursuit, isolating themselves in forests and caves, and practicing terrible austerities. At times, they pulled their hair out in frustration or pounded the forest floor in desperation. Don't fool yourself into imagining that you are going to have it any easier. Just like them, you will need guts to carry on in the face of a crisis.

Crises can be physical, emotional, mental, or any combination of them at once. A participant came to me during his first Enlightenment Intensive, and I tell you he was a fireball. His skin was flushed red, and I could feel the heat radiating off him. He said, "I've got a fever, a bad fever."

I asked, "Did you come to the intensive this way?" He answered, "No, the fever came on after I got here. I must have picked up a bug." I continued, "You weren't this way when you came, so I think you should stay with the technique." He pushed back against my suggestion that his condition had anything to do with the enlightenment process, saying, "You know, diseases have incubation periods."

Although I felt it was a mistake, I let him lay down. Half an hour later, he walked back in the room and said, "I can't believe it. You were right. As soon as I got away from the technique, the fever went away. It just faded out."

Within minutes of resuming his contemplation, his fever was back in full force. He got even hotter, and his eyes became bloodshot, but nothing could stop him now. He came out the other side of this crisis and the fever passed. Later in the intensive, he had an enlightenment experience.

That's a physical crisis, but the exact same thing happens with the mind and emotions. There is no telling in advance what your symptoms will be. Everyone's got their song and dance. You might feel emotionally distraught and start to cry. You may get so scared that you start to shake. You might grow angry, furious, or depressed. Mental crises are more a matter of being undermined by attitudes that arise from beneath the conscious mind. You might think, "I can't do it," or "I'm no good," or "I don't deserve it."

You may feel inadequate and blame yourself, "Why should I try when I always fail anyway?" You might grow indignant and blame the external circumstances, "There's not enough time for me to process everything that's happening, and I just can't risk going forward with this." You might be very suave and avoid blaming anyone or anything, "I can see how this is great for other people, but I'm a different kind of person, one that can't get enlightened, and this is just not my cup of tea."

It's fairly common to feel that if you stick with the technique you are going to cease to exist or physically die. Although less common, you might become afraid of going insane and think, "If I go on, I'll flip out completely." You might fear that your life will change fundamentally. I remember one woman saying, "Oh my God, I can't go on with this. I'll leave my husband, because I won't be able to stand being a housewife if I know who I really am."

All these ideas and feelings seem very real because you're so identified with them. In the throes of a crisis, you can't see they are just ideas and feelings.

You will only get into a crisis if you have committed to some goal. If you don't have a goal, the moment any real difficulty arises you will just say, "forget it," and avoid the crisis by backing off the technique. A crisis is actually a good sign, and it's important that you have this perspective. You are not trying to avoid barriers and crises; you are trying to get through them.

When the physical symptoms, emotional reactions, and mental invalidations begin, just know that you are coming up against a crisis. The mind is a total fraud. Once you call its bluff, the crisis disappears every time. If you are determined to go ahead anyway, the fever will abate, the emotional storm pass, and the dilemma resolve.

If you stick with the technique as given, you will open doors to rooms that are pitch dark inside. You will hear monsters roaring and be afraid to enter. But the moment you resolve to walk into that room, the mind has already been defeated, and the monsters will be seen as just illusions.

Chapter Seven
Barriers to Enlightenment

Along with knowing how to get through a crisis, there are common barriers to enlightenment that must be overcome.

Most of these barriers boil down to a single great barrier: not persisting with the technique. It doesn't matter whether the cause is boredom, distraction, low self-esteem, fear of failure, resistance to hard work, poor physical or mental health, phenomena, or whatever. If the result is backing off the technique, you have fallen into the trap that defeats more aspirants than any other.

Preconceived ideas are a major barrier to enlightenment. Their power lies in that they are unconscious and go unnoticed. Instead of a preconception, you see it as an obvious truth and something not worth questioning.

Our minds are filled with these preconceived ideas. You might stake your life on the fact that the sun rises in the east and sets in the west. It's obvious; how could anyone deny it? Yet it is true only from the limited point of view of a person on earth. All relative truths are based on viewpoints like this. When you are going for the absolute truth of enlightenment, in which relative points of view cease to exist, you have to abandon all preconceived ideas.

For example, say you are working on the question, "What am I?" You might assume that what you are is a physical thing. Or you may think of yourself as located somewhere in time and space. While relatively true, these ideas may not be absolutely true.

As long as your contemplation is based on preconceptions like this, you are not being open to all possibilities. You have unconsciously placed a limit on your contemplation and will see only what falls into your presumed categories.

Religious convictions are a type of preconceived idea imbued with special significance. You may hang onto these ideas out of family loyalty, fear, or guilt. Your life may have been benefited from a particular teacher or tradition, and you may feel an allegiance to them. You or others may revere these ideas as the direct knowledge of divinely inspired prophets and spiritual masters.

But enlightenment has nothing to do with beliefs, convictions, or someone else's realization. A religious conviction is just a preconceived idea and not the truth itself. The solution to all preconceived ideas, even the most dearly held ones, is to set them aside as soon as you notice them, so you can be open to your own experience of truth.

Avoidance is another major barrier, as there are a million different ways to avoid facing up to the truth. Most of the time, you won't have a clue about what you are doing. You'll just find yourself going through the motions half-heartedly, unaware you are avoiding anything at all.

Letting yourself get distracted by external things is one example. You may become overly concerned with the environment, "I need a different seat; it's too hot in here; I'm hungry," that kind of thing. Sexual or romantic feelings can be a powerful distraction and way to avoid the rigor of doing the technique. The solution is to set all outside concerns aside. Face the object of your contemplation, and channel your frustration or passion into the technique.

Some people believe they are only making progress if they are screaming, crying and emoting all over the place. It's not true, and this is just another form of avoidance. You may go through strong emotions or even outbursts, but don't go off the technique to get involved in emotional releasing. Let yourself be emotionally open, but it is an error to indulge in emotions beyond communicating the intensity of what occurs as a result of your contemplation.

You might also avoid by intellectualizing. If you find yourself thinking incessantly, or getting lost in stories, you should focus on contemplating more deeply. Ignore anything in your mind that doesn't occur as a direct result of your contemplation. Or you might avoid by turning inward to contemplate, hiding out in your inner search for truth. The solution here is to communicate more actively, getting across to your partner whatever came up as a result of your contemplation.*

Guilt can be a barrier, and I've seen people do the technique well and come right to the edge of enlightenment and hang there for hours, holding themselves back. If you feel in your heart that you have done wrong and not treated people well, you may be afraid that you will misuse the power of certainty that enlightenment brings, which holds a lot of sway in the world.

There are several ways to handle this barrier. One is to decide to be good to people starting now. That commitment, if sincere,

---

*In solo contemplation, the solution is to not sit passively in meditation. Be active in your technique, intending to directly experience yourself as you truly are, registering whatever arises in your field of awareness as a result, and then recycling through the technique.

47

will do the trick. Another is to know that enlightenment brings with it the capacity to do things well and treat people better; it's automatic. Still another is to realize that becoming enlightened is actually a great service, as you will be more able to help relieve the suffering of others.

The last way to handle this is to thrash about, moaning and groaning, lifetime after lifetime, holding yourself back from the truth, success and happiness until you feel that you have paid your debt and wiped the slate clean.

There is no "law of karma" in the universe that pertains to enlightenment. In fact, enlightenment destroys karma, totally. Yet if you decide that you need to suffer to absolve yourself from some wrong done, there is no technique that can force you to grow. I'd suggest you take a different approach, however, by opening up to enlightenment.

Fear is another major barrier. When working on "Who am I?" you may feel afraid that who you really are will be disappointing, shameful, or unacceptable to others. If you have an investment in being a certain way, for example a "nice guy," you may be afraid of discovering that you are ultimately not that way.

As contemplation deepens, you might grow afraid that your life will change fundamentally if you allow yourself to go any further. You might become a powerful person, or a saint, or just something very different than what you are used to being. The solution in all these cases is to face the fear and experience the truth of who you are.

Confronting the fear of death is common and there are various levels of this fear. Whether it's the demise of the physical body, the death of the ego-oriented personality, or ceasing to identify with anything located in space and time, you may feel terrified or desperate. I've had many people cry out, "It's not my ego that is dying, it's me! Don't you understand?" This feeling of terror is a tremendous barrier.

There is always some risk in enlightenment work. There is a gap between the unenlightened and enlightened states, a void in which you cease to exist. It is a timeless instant, and there is no way to bridge that gap without taking the leap. The solution is to want the truth enough that you are willing to die and cease to exist. There is no other way through it. While I've never seen anyone die at this juncture, you could die, so there can be no guarantees.

Overlooking the obvious is a subtle barrier. For some reason, you refuse to see what is really occurring for you. This becomes a barrier to contemplation when the same thing keeps coming up over and over, and it won't go away. If this occurs, you are probably overlooking some part of your experience and failing to acknowledge and communicate what is occurring as a result of your contemplation.*

Maybe your thoughts are clear, but you are avoiding the accompanying emotional intensity because it is uncomfortable. Perhaps you censor out sex or violence because your mother wouldn't approve of those feelings, which have been shut down since childhood. You might be afraid of the consequences of owning and saying how it really is for you. For whatever reason, you are overlooking the obvious and your contemplation bogs down as a result.

*In solo contemplation, the solution is to investigate deeper and register the full scope of what is arising in your contemplation.

Over-wanting enlightenment can be a barrier. It's not a bad thing to desperately want the truth, but putting all your energy into wanting will not get you there. You could want to be enlightened for eons and still never make it. You have to use the technique to get through the barriers. The solution is to channel your wanting into doing the technique correctly.

The body can be a barrier to enlightenment. My observation over the years is that people who take care of their bodies, who have better health in general, are aided in their search for enlightenment.

Caffeine, cigarettes, alcohol, drugs, chemical exposure, overeating or poor food choices, exercising too little, all these things contribute to a toxified body and mind. If the body is aching, and the mind is thick and cloudy, it's easy to wander off the technique.

If you have physical or mental health issues, you may want to take a longer term approach. Begin your path with healing and growth activities. If you keep at it, you will make it to the place where enlightenment work is appropriate.

Real progress is made when you ignore all the distractions, face all the guilt and fears, and open yourself to the direct experience of truth. This kind of openness is genuine and not mechanical.

Anything mechanical like regulating your breathing, controlling your thoughts, trying to figure things out, or applying a technique to release your feelings will just rearrange your mind. It will never give you the fundamental change in consciousness that results from the direct experience of yourself as you truly are.

Chapter Eight
The Final Barrier of Phenomena

There are a few barriers that only occur near the onset of an enlightenment experience. The mind is a great seducer, and I doubt there's ever been an aspirant who made it straight through these barriers the first time. Almost everyone gets distracted, tricked, fascinated, or horrified by the phenomena attendant to the enlightenment process.

These phenomena tend to come on after you've spent some time dealing with a barrier called no-man's land. Your mind is blank. It's been cleared out by doing the technique, but you persist in looking and trying to see or locate yourself. You have this experience of peering out into space, with nothing occurring as a result of your contemplation, sometimes for hours and hours.

Having a blank mind is not enlightenment, but it is a stage in the enlightenment process. To get through the desert of no-man's land, you have to stick with the technique, even in the face of this "nothing happening" phase. Give up trying to see, feel, or perceive yourself in any way. Continue to intend to directly experience yourself, tolerating the nothingness, and remaining open to whatever occurs in your consciousness as a result of that intention.

There is another stage in the enlightenment process that can act like a barrier I call "meditation." This is when all your attention becomes concentrated and fixated on one thing. If working on "Who am I?" you might get some sense of yourself and hold right there. In the moment, you'll probably think you are doing the technique correctly, but you are not.

Having a concentrated mind is also not enlightenment. You will make progress meditating, and many people have gotten enlightened this way, but it takes about two or three years.* It's better to contemplate by intending to directly experience the object of your enlightenment, remaining open, and communicating what comes up to your partner.

At this point of concentration or blank mindedness, various phenomena may arise to distract you. How many innocent aspirants have been sidetracked by these fascinating distractions?

These phenomena can take any form, and the closer you get to enlightenment the more intense they get. You can often feel them coming on. There will be a rush of energy through the body. The mind will say, "Oh my God, it's happening."

The body may start to jerk, jump, or roll around on the floor. Heat may flash through, or chills, or tears. Emotions may rush to the surface. You may fall into comforting states of bliss, insight, or have visions. The mind may catch fire, go off like fireworks, or be lost in a flash of white light. You may gain psychic abilities or remember past lives. While at least a surprised, "Oh!" is usually uttered, there might be hardly any phenomena at all.

There is no predicting the form phenomena will take. That's determined by whatever impurity or blockage is impeding your

---

* Technically, Yogeshwar did not consider meditation one of the final barriers to enlightenment. He saw it as an acceptable variation of the technique. I've included this clear distinction between meditation and contemplation here because of its importance for solo contemplators.

arrival at the enlightened state. While fascinating, phenomena are not important in themselves. They do not produce enlightenment, nor is the occurrence of dramatic phenomena evidence that you're enlightened.

In Zen these phenomena are called *makyo*, which means "the devil" or "diabolical," because they lure aspirants away from the truth. Phenomena are not bad; the difficulty is the distraction they pose. The enlightened state approaches; the phenomenon happens, and you get distracted.

The right response is simply to ignore the phenomena. You don't chase after phenomena and try to make anything happen. You don't resist or try to stop the phenomena from happening. You don't take any action one way or another with regards to whatever is occurring. You go right on doing the technique and ignore the phenomena.

The content of the unconscious mind is almost always dramatic because it's full of intensity that wasn't fully experienced and is now arising to be completed. That's why you should not stop the phenomena. If you stop it, you shut down the whole process. But you should not think, "Now I see what I should do. I should yell and scream and make phenomena happen."

There are appropriate times to do primal therapy, bioenergetics, and other techniques that willfully bring on phenomena of one kind or another. For enlightenment, you should continue to intend to directly experience yourself, and remain open to whatever occurs in your consciousness as a result of that intention.

Interestingly enough, even if you get through all the barriers, you can still get distracted by phenomena that continue after the enlightenment experience. Post enlightenment, you may want to say, "I know the Truth, white light is pouring out of me, and I have come!" In Zen, this "after glow" is called the *stink of enlightenment* because it's just more phenomena and not enlightened consciousness itself.

I'd say about half of the gurus today are in this state. They've had some real experience of Truth but were seduced by the phenomena that accompanied or followed it.

Teachers who succumbed to this and later returned to their spiritual practice often look back and laugh. "I was just crazy," they'll say. At the time, they took their messianic feelings seriously, and the people around them might have too.

My standard is that if you have an enlightenment experience and everybody in the world is not enlightened along with you in fifteen minutes, you have more work to do and should see to it.

Chapter Nine
Getting Inside the Palace of Truth

Here's a story I used to tell to illustrate the difficulty involved in the final step to enlightenment. Imagine that someone comes to you from this marvelous place, the Palace of Absolute Truth. After listening to him talk, you say, "I'd like to visit this palace myself. How do I get there?" He says, "Well, there are a number of different paths, but if you will just follow this one of contemplation, it will lead you there. I'll be your guide."

You decide to go for it and begin your trek immediately. You travel through the valley of memories and scale the mountain of the intellect and crags of personal convictions. You enter the complex land of emotionality, enduring its extremes. "Oh boy, I feel great," and, "Oh God, why did I ever embark on this trip? I want to go home." You persevere despite distractions and the obscuring fog of drowsiness. You wade through the waterfalls of hallucination.

Then you enter the expansive desert of no-man's land, wandering and calling out, "Where is this palace?" You'd give up at this point, except you've come so far that it's not worth turning back now. Besides, your guide keeps whispering in your ear, "The palace is just a little bit farther over that rise."

You finally cross the desert and enter the forest of longlastingness. Suddenly, there in the clearing ahead, is the palace. Upon seeing it you say, "Ohhhh, it is beautiful," and you think maybe you've gotten the Truth, but your guide says, "No, this is not Truth; this is just its outer wrapping. This is the appearance of Truth." You reply, "But I'm so blown out!" He says, "Keep on going."

So off you go, and you're getting closer and closer to the palace. Arriving at its exterior wall, you touch it and say, "I've never felt anything like this. Not only does it look beautiful; it feels blissful." But your guide says, "Yes, but that's not like being inside the palace. If you want the absolute, direct Truth of enlightenment, you must get inside the palace"

"Okay," you say, "I'm ready." Walking around the palace, you don't see any entrance. There's no door, no drawbridge, not even a window. There just doesn't seem to be any way to get inside. "Well, I'm going inside anyway," you say. So you kick the wall, and then claw it with your fingernails. You even bite it with your teeth. All your efforts are to no avail. So you back off about a hundred yards, put your head down, and you make a mad dash at the wall. Splat!

In desperation, you ask the guide, "How do I get inside?" The guide says, 'There's no how. That wall is a total barrier. Doing more of anything that you did to get to the Palace of Absolute Truth won't get you inside, no matter how hard you try. There's nothing you can do."

You say, "Well, I've come this far, now what?" The guide continues, "I suggest you sit down and calmly contemplate the inside of the palace. Intend to be inside the palace – inside, not outside.

"All right," you say, and a few minutes later you report back, "I did what you said and nothing happened. I want to get me an axe!"

I want to pause the story at this point and talk about this last step, and offer some guidance on how you can handle this impossible situation you're in.

I've talked about the various kinds of phenomena, and it's when you're facing this impenetrable wall that they will arise to distract you. Along with the full spectrum of phenomena, you may get mental images of what it's like inside the palace. There's a danger that you will convince yourself those images are enlightenment. Even if your mental images are right, projecting that you know something is not the same as being inside the Palace of Absolute Truth.

The solution here is to face the fact that you don't know. It might be pure bliss. It might be like being on a torture rack. It might be neither of those preconceived ideas, just a grey expanse. The truth is that you'll never know for sure until it's your direct experience. Right now, you don't know and being open to that unknown is the only thing that makes it possible to get inside the palace.

Even if you've had an enlightenment experience before, getting to the next level of enlightenment is the same thing all over again. You encounter this wall, which may also occur to you as a chasm separating you from Truth. That chasm is only crossed by what could be called grace, a leap of faith, or good fortune. It always entails a discontinuity, a break between states with no apparent connection.

When you hit the seemingly impenetrable wall of the palace of truth, you will know that you've come up against something significant. It's not enlightenment, as there's no glow to it, and nothing has happened that means anything to you. Yet it's clear that you're up against something different than all your previous layers of confusion and identification. At this point, do what your guide says. Intend to have conscious, direct knowledge of yourself as you truly are. Just intend, just be open, and either it happens or it doesn't.

Enlightenment is not complex. Traveling through all the difficult and comfortable territory to get to the wall of the palace of truth may be complicated, but the enlightenment experience itself is always the purest simplicity possible. There is no complexity possible in absolute truth. Even the concept of simplicity doesn't apply to it.

You might be the kind of person who has a high IQ and can't stand uncomplicated situations. You've got to make everything difficult and hard. I was one of those smart types, and I ground myself into little bits and pieces trying to get enlightened through the intellect. Don't be tempted into the trap of complexity. Try not to form preconceived ideas. Try not to complexify.

To one degree or another, everyone will end up stymied outside the Palace of Absolute Truth. There's no avoiding it. Emphasize the second part of the technique, just being open to whatever may occur. And by the grace of the Absolute Truth, either you'll be sitting inside or sitting outside the palace, but at least you won't be battering your brains out anymore.

Listen when your guide says, "You don't have to strain to do this. Keep at it steadily, but you don't have to suffer. Remain determined to get enlightened, but stop straining the brain and mind by trying to force the situation."

Most of the journey to enlightenment is finding out who you are not. But de-identification is not enough. You must have conscious, direct knowledge of the one who is left after all the de-identification.

Some people strip themselves so bare they are like a shining nothing, but they are still not conscious of that which remains.

Do not confuse total de-identification with enlightenment. There is still one more step. It takes a tremendous determination to stay with the technique through to the very end. It is awesomely hard to do, but also simple, and it's the only way to enter the Palace of Absolute Truth.

Chapter Ten
Levels of Enlightenment

There are not different kinds of enlightenment. There is not a blue enlightenment, a red enlightenment, and a pink enlightenment. There are different depths or levels of enlightenment, but these are not ultimate distinctions

You could say there's a spectrum from zero conscious, direct knowledge of yourself to total conscious, direct knowledge of yourself as you truly are. The first glimmer you get are these flash experiences.* While you could include them in some very minimalist definition of enlightenment, they are shallow and temporary. What you want is to move on to deeper and more stable enlightenments.

The first level that can be properly called enlightenment is the direct experience of who you are. To arrive at this "who level" of enlightenment, you must de-identify from false and mistaken notions of who you are until you arrive at the direct experience of the one you actually are.

This realization is always the same, and it makes it clear "which one" you are. "I am me" is the most common report. While this enlightenment is relatively shallow, it is critical for your continued growth.

Once you know who you are, you can shift to the question "What am I?" and the de-identification process will continue. You may de-identify from your body, and in the gap that opens in the moment of de-identification have a touch of direct experience.

* Somewhat like the experience produced by the self-discovery Cat Exercise on page 27.

Your fall from that momentary enlightenment will occur almost instantaneously, often too quickly to be noticed. Something will pop into your mind, and you will unconsciously latch onto another level of identification. You might come out saying, "What I am is spirit," and it will occur as a revelation because you did in fact have a direct experience.

You will go through a whole progression of de-identifications and re-identifications like this, which tend to occur in a general order due to the structure of the mind. You may think you are a body or a brain, various thoughts and ideas, a personality or cluster of sub-personalities, then different layers and powers of the psyche.

When you begin to de-identify from the more basic viewpoints, you are likely to start oscillating between thinking of yourself as something and nothing. You'll come out of direct knowing and say, "I'm nothing." The next time, you'll say, "I'm everything."*

This process goes on and on as you de-identify from perceptual viewpoints, matter, energy, space, time, and existence itself. While this is happening, your relative level of enlightenment can be measured by your degree of identification with any thing or idea that you are not.

You eventually become totally de-identified, and you could call this level of enlightenment the steady state. It is stable and does not come and go. It comes about if you have been in the enlightened state for twenty minutes to two hours. Before you reach steady state, your enlightenment is subject to remission.

*The re-identification that follows on the heels of a direct experience is usually an approximate opposite of whatever you just de-identified from.

61

This is because you are still identified with something or nothing, and thus can be influenced by external factors and pressures. As your enlightenment stabilizes, your conscious, direct knowledge returns more quickly when outside influences are lifted. Eventually it can be restored at will.

The mind keeps getting stripped until even its basic framework falls away. Then your relationship to all other beings becomes self-evident and over time grows crystal clear. Through this you gain the capacity to see what actions are needed in any situation to bring about fulfillment for everyone.

Language begins to falter here. It's enough to say that you gradually become free of neurosis and compulsivity, and able to live without thought and by presence alone. This is the definition of liberation that I favor.

The story of the blind men and the elephant is an analogy for the seemingly endless succession of partial experiences that occur along the way to enlightenment. Five blind men find an elephant. One feels a leg of the elephant and says it is like a tree. One feels the tail and says it is like a rope. One grabs the trunk and says it is like a snake. One touches the ear and says it is like a leaf, and one leans against the elephant's side and says it is like a wall.

While all five have truly touched the ultimate, they describe it differently based on their relative point of view. They argue on and on about it because each is convinced he's right, which in a way is true. Fortunately, there's an end to this conflict and controversy. When you see the whole elephant, you are finished with regards to enlightenment contemplation.

Chapter Ten
Integrating Life Into Enlightenment

After an experience of Absolute Truth, people find themselves back in the relative world and a society that is not functioning in harmony with what they now know is actually true. This often leads them to ask, "How can I integrate enlightenment into my life?" A better approach might be to ask the question differently, "How can I integrate my life into enlightenment?"

People often have the idea that enlightenment is the end of the road. You have this mountain top experience and live happily ever after. This romantic notion ignores the fact that most enlightenments are partial, and attachments, identifications, and ignorance remain. Any incompletion tends to pull you back into life as you ordinarily experience it.

If you want to go beyond having a few enlightenment experiences, you will be faced with the challenge of entering a whole new way of living. In this respect, enlightenment is actually a beginning because it gives you the opportunity to bring your life into harmony with the Truth you have now experienced.

Transforming your life is a lifetime project. But manifesting your enlightenment completely is all that's left to do after enlightenment. You don't have to make this choice. You can be happy with the intrinsic benefits of your experience and return to your life as before, more able to live from who you actually are instead of a fake persona. There is nothing bad or wrong about this, but it may be dissatisfying if you want to keep your process of spiritual growth going.

If you make a sincere decision to embark on this path of life transformation, any parts of your body, mind or emotional make-up that are blocking your full expression of the Truth will come to the forefront of your consciousness to be cleared up. You'd think that fighting your way through the Pandora's box of your mind to have a direct experience of Truth would be enough, but this post-enlightenment purification is a whole new process.

How does a full manifestation of enlightenment come about? It can only come about through surrender to Truth or God or Love. There's a catch here. In order to surrender, you have to find some Absolute to surrender to. That's the value of willful techniques like Enlightenment Intensives, which give you the direct experience of Truth needed to practice surrender.

To continue to grow spiritually, it is necessary to treat others well. Treating others well is not a moral imperative; it is a question of behaving consistently with the truth of how things actually are. I'm not trying to sell you on ethics. I'm just reporting the results of a lifetime of intensive research into this enlightenment business. If you don't incorporate ethical behavior into your life, you'll hit a ceiling and not be able to go on in your enlightenment work in any meaningful way.

What is ethical behavior? Every religion has guidelines. The ten commandments of Judaism and Yoga's yama and niyama are examples. Christ said to love your neighbor as yourself. These guidelines were not created by misguided souls trying to control people. They are descriptions of how a person behaves after manifesting enlightenment completely. If you want to live consistently with your enlightenment, they will help you work toward what will be the end result.

It says in the Hindu scriptures that the world will be saved by people with tears running down their cheeks, voices choked with emotion, telling of their love for each other. I believe that.

You can tell if your life is becoming more consistent with your enlightenment by asking yourself the following questions. Are you growing in the capacity to enjoy yourself and experience pleasure without guilt? Are your family and other relationships harmonious? Are you prospering materially and otherwise? Are you treating other people better?

If you are making real progress in these areas, not just in appearance but in actual fact, then you are successfully integrating your life into enlightenment.*

*This concludes part one of this book on Enlightenment Contemplation. The next chapter begins part two and its exposition of Natural Meditation.

Surrender the Relative

Surrender the relative
into the Absolute,
love releasing into love.
Find what is changeless,
whole, and free,
and give the reins
of your life over
to that mystery.
Nothing is lost or
defeated when you
surrender to what's real.
It may feel like you are
losing yourself,
but you actually gain
the universe.

Danna Faulds

Chapter Twelve
Value and Limits of Willful Practice

People serious about their growth are driven time and time again into the realm of peak experience. Whether via this technique, or that workshop, this meditation approach, or that drug, they inevitably fall back again. This is because the enlightened state cannot be willfully maintained.

Willful techniques, including the ones I developed, can only take you so far. They can help you get yourself together physically, mentally, and emotionally. You can use them to improve your life. They can even produce a touch of the Truth. But as soon as desire arises, and the will is reactivated, you lose that depth. Only through openness and surrender can enlightenment be continually experienced.

If you are a serious and dedicated student of personal growth, you must ask yourself: How can I get past the limitations of a temporary peak experience? For twenty-five years, night and day, I used willful technique after willful technique. I grew a lot, realized a lot, and encountered the Truth many times. I even stopped calling it Truth and started calling it God. Yet deep down I knew that I was only crawling forward inch by inch on a path that would take lifetimes.

It was at this time that I met my spiritual teacher, Swami Kripalu. He immediately understood why I could not grow rapidly. I will share with you the practice of surrender meditation that he taught me.

This is not to say willful techniques have no value because they do. Almost every aspirant needs them for two reasons. First, it's impossible to surrender until you have found an Absolute somewhere in your life. Willful techniques like Enlightenment Intensive contemplation enable you to directly experience the Truth. This is essential because it gives you something to which you can surrender.

Secondly, once you surrender, a natural purification process will begin. This is a little like a child who has been playing out in the dirt and his mother wants to give him a bath. Getting in the tub and being scrubbed clean is uncomfortable at first. If you have a lot of toxins in your body, it may react very strongly. The purification may even grow so intense that you are not able to tolerate it and as a result stop your practice.

Because of this, you should start Natural Meditation after adequate preparation.* Toxins accumulate when you eat a bad diet, breathe polluted air, smoke cigarettes, drink coffee, and use alcohol and drugs. Willful practices like good diet, deep breathing, hatha yoga, aerobic exercise, and techniques that clear the mind and emotions help prepare you to practice surrender.

Where willful techniques leave off, the realm of surrender begins. If surrender is commenced in a relatively pure state, it can be like throwing a match into dry tinder. Your purification process will blaze up to quickly consume the remaining impurities. For those who are ready, the path of Natural Meditation is open if they so choose!

*Along with Enlightenment Intensives, Yogeshwar developed and taught an extensive body of teachings and techniques called Holistic Yoga that was designed help students purify, grow, develop life mastery, and prepare for the practice of Natural Meditation.

Chapter Thirteen
What is Surrender?

Before meeting my guru, I had spent years trying to sort out the best way to reach the happiest and most liberated life. I had assembled a list of fifty excellent methods of working with the body and mind.

The list included massage, energy work, Feldenkreis, yoga, pranayama, bioenergetics, fasting, good diet, primal scream, Gestalt therapy, Reichian therapy, trauma release, mind clearing, communication dyads, dream work, prayer, meditation, chanting, and many others. I was developing an assessment test so everyone who came to my growth center could be directed to what their body, emotional system, and mind needed most.

Then Swami Kripalu taught me Natural Meditation, in which all you do is surrender to Truth and the exact things happen with the exact intensity to accomplish exactly what is needed for you.

"What a relief," I thought. "If I can learn to surrender, the Truth itself will guide my meditation and my growth will continue naturally, without any need for me to know anything or plan ahead. This is a Godsend!"

Now I can speak not from theory but from experience. What Swami Kripalu taught me is in fact the case. Surrender will lead you on the most fascinating, exciting, sometimes boring, and other times terrifying journey to the feet of the Divine.

You might ask, "If it's so easy, why doesn't everybody do Natural Meditation?" I've already mentioned two barriers.

You must have already found some Absolute in your life, and you need to be prepared to tolerate the purification that results from surrendering. But there is something beyond those two obstacles.

Most people are firmly attached to their ego. They want to be in charge and make things happen. They want to be the doer and enjoy the fruits of their actions. This is the ordinary way of proceeding in life, and it works to a degree.

The ego sits back and says, "Look at me. See what I'm doing. See what I did!" Yet in truth, it is Nature that does all things and none of us are at cause. The act of surrender is simply the gradual realization of this.

There is a very simple way to test this truth of non-doing. Affirm you won't move a finger, think a thought, or breathe. Within a few moments, you'll be moving, thinking and breathing again. Only it wasn't you who started back, because it wasn't you doing it in the first place. Nature causes the body to breathe, the brain to think, and hunger to come.

If you are strongly identified with being the doer, surrender will not occur and the approach of Natural Meditation will not work for you. Everyone has an ego; this is not the problem. If you want to resist and fight, surrender will not work. If you are willing to yield some of your doership, the doorway is open.

Surrender is so central to Natural Meditation that it deserves careful clarification. The technique is not very complicated, but you need to clearly understand what surrender is, who is surrendering, and to what you are surrendering.

The dictionary defines surrender as the opposite of victory, or defeat. This is not what is meant in Natural Meditation. You might say that surrender is letting things be the way they truly are. Instead of using your will to make things the way you want, you surrender and let them be.*

To understand who surrenders, you must ask questions like: Who am I? What am I? What is this life? Is there anything here that is Absolute, or is it all relative and changing? Am I this body, these feelings, this mind and ego personality? Or is there something independent of the body, feelings, and my mind-based identity?

You, the true individual, are the one with the free will needed to surrender. You can choose to resist life, or you can choose to surrender and let things be.

It's not natural for the body or mind to surrender anything, to anyone, under any circumstances. They are programmed for survival. In humanity's tenure on earth, this programming has not produced anything beyond temporary pleasure and a measure of material security. It is you, the one who has the power of choice, who can choose to entertain another way.

Surrendering what you truly are is an impossibility. You can only let go of something that is not really you. However you do have a certain locus of control over your body and mind.

*This is the first step and cutting edge of Natural Meditation's method of surrender. Just because it is simply stated, don't minimize its importance. Choosing to let things be as they truly are will reveal and uproot all your strategies to control, fix, milk something from, deny and defend yourself from reality. It will compel you to give up you active war or passive stand-off with the truth.

You are the boss; you have dominion and power.* This control is what you surrender. You are not surrendering your Self; you are surrendering anything that occurs in your body, mind and feelings as a result of your choice to surrender.

There is a story about a street person who stood staring at a shiny parked car long enough to convince himself that it was his. All day long, pedestrians walked by and he would greet them, "Look at my new Mercedes Benz."

The ego is like this. It's convinced that it owns your body, heart, mind, memories, knowledge, power of judgment, intuition, and life. Somewhere along the way in Natural Meditation, you have the incredible realization that you deluded yourself into thinking these things were ever yours to begin with.

In Natural Meditation, you not only surrender. You surrender to something Absolute. You turn control over to something you respect and feel comfortable placing your full reliance upon. There are many ways to think about the Ultimate, and different words can be used. I've used the term Truth, meaning the way things actually are, but you can think of it in whatever way has meaning for you. You can call it God, Goddess, Divine Love, the Sacred, Perfection, or the Cosmic Finality.

You might think surrender is not doing anything. You'll just lie down and nothing will take place. This is incorrect. Things will happen in your body, mind and feelings. You surrender your body and all your mental machinations to God. You let the mind, body and feelings do what they do, or don't do, as moved by the Divine hand.

*As meditation deepens, you discover even this modest locus of control is less definite than imagined and ultimately illusory.

Surrender then is letting the Truth, the way things really are, guide your meditation. It's as if you say, "Here Truth, here God, this body is yours, this mind is yours. Do with them what you want." You quit using your will; you quit controlling.
You give dominion over to an Ultimate that you respect enough to do so. In giving it over, you are unburdened of the whole project and free to go into union.

This divine union is the ultimate outcome of surrender. Your own True Nature comes into union with Truth or God. The scriptures say it is like pouring milk into milk. These two, which are both divine, are now in union. While a long-term project, this is the promise of Natural Meditation.

Surrender Prayer

Lord, I give you my body.
I give you my mind.
I give you my heart,
knowing that
my soul is already
in your safekeeping.

Danna Faulds

Chapter Fourteen
Surrender Only to God

Before meeting Swami Kripalu, I had studied religion. Surrender seemed weak to me, a consolation for the defeated, and an avoidance of personal responsibility. Yet Swami Kripalu was a religious man whose bearing called my assumptions into question. He was clearly a winner, someone who had been victorious in life.

I asked, "Master, tell me how this works?" Swami Kripalu told me that there is an Absolute that is other than you.* If there is nothing other than you, there is nothing to surrender to and the whole principle of surrender is nonsense. You can say, "I surrender to myself," but that's just illogical gibberish.

Surrender is turning control over to this Absolute. If there is nothing that you love, trust, respect, can rely upon, or think about as Ultimate or Perfect, you should not take up surrender. Keep searching and using willful methods until you find something you can genuinely trust.

If you surrender to anything and everything you will get into trouble. If you surrender to your body, mind, and feelings, your desires will run wild and this can lead to uncontrolled and anti-social behavior. Taken to an extreme, your whole life can become one big profligate mess, like Jim Morrison or even Charles Manson.

Do not surrender to the pains or urges of the body. Do not surrender to desire and strong emotions. Do not surrender to resistance, paranoia, and stories in your mind. Choose to

*There is no duality in the Absolute, but it can be approached via self or other.

75

surrender all these things to the Highest. Can you see the difference?

Surrender only to God. This one principle will save you pain and difficulties beyond measure. Surrender only to Perfection, and let Him, or Her, or It resolve all your problems and impurities. If you have some vagueness about exactly what It is, so be it, that's okay. But do not surrender to anything else. This will keep you out of trouble.

Some people are prone to falling into the trap of surrendering to spirits, lights, and things that go bump in the night. Do not surrender to spirit guides or space people. It may seem like I'm joking, but this is a serious point. The only practitioner I've ever seen get in trouble with this method insisted on surrendering to spirits. I pulled her out of it several times, but she kept going back. Eventually, she had a psychotic break. This is not Natural Meditation.

Surrender is a profound choice, and if you choose to surrender, the purification process begins immediately, whether you like it or not. Perhaps for a time you will think you are receiving important messages from the spirit realm to deliver to humanity. Such phenomena may occur in your meditation. Well and good, let it happen, but remain aware that this is just a stage you are going through, and part of the purifying madness that occurs for everyone. Let it pass by. Do not fall prey to grandiosity and other distractions. Surrender only to Truth.

People practicing surrender sometimes run into trouble in their relationships outside of the meditation room, and this principle of surrendering only to the Highest applies there too. Love does not mean surrendering to other people's personalities, weaknesses, neurotic demands, and nonsense. You will destroy each other with such misguided actions. Surrender only to the Divine Truth in the heart of everyone. This is the act of love.

For example, if someone is complaining to me about this or that, I may choose to ignore their complaints. I am not ignoring him or her as an individual. I am choosing to ignore the neurosis that is looking to me for validation. Natural Meditation brings the bliss of love and saintly behavior with regard to others, without you trying to be that way.

If you learn surrender, you won't have to say, "How should I treat this complaining person? That's right, I should not get angry." Your anger will be surrendered and naturally transformed into divine love. Saintly behavior will occur because who you are is open-hearted, naturally, and you will find a way to respond without giving in to their neurotic needs.

It's impractical to say to yourself, "Surrender everything, fully, instantaneously." That's too heavy and won't work. Instead, you should say, "Go into your meditation room, sit down, and surrender your body, mind and feelings to the Ultimate for one hour. Just do your best, and when you come out take control of your life again." This degree of surrender is workable and allows you to persist with it day after day and make steady progress.

Once you understand the basics, surrender is not so much a matter of knowing how. It's a matter of how brave you are. As you open up to the Truth, every self-delusion, pretense, suppressed hurt, resisted experience, and trick you have played comes to the surface and exposes itself. Fortunately, once they are experienced God removes them. She brings them up. She takes them away, and they are dissolved and gone forever.

77

Chapter Fifteen
Releasing the Life Energy

In our society, it is not considered very important to use your heart. I believe that deep down everyone would like to feel more loved and able to love, but we've learned to rely on our heads. This has brought us material prosperity, but it's also made us hardhearted and thwarted the love, peace, and high consciousness we also want.

Natural Meditation is a method of surrender that opens the heart by releasing the life energy that's been captured by the mind. As the energy begins to stream, things cease to feel hollow and pointless. As you continue to surrender, you discover this energy has a remarkable intelligence and evolutionary power. It knows what you need. Spontaneously and automatically, your growth unfolds. That's really all there is to say. The rest is doing it.

You cannot figure your way into releasing this energy. The more you use your will, the more firmly it is trapped. Nor can you open up and let the life energy run wild. This desire will want this, and that desire will want that, and you'll get into all sorts of difficulties trying to fulfill them. Natural Meditation teaches you how to safely liberate the suppressed life energy by surrendering it to Truth or God.

When I speak about life energy, I am not talking about some mysterious thing. I am talking about the most ordinary thing. It's the aspect of nature that empowers the universe, not only making it run in orderly patterns but also giving it an evolutionary direction. From the very beginning of creation to the very end, everything happens through this intelligent energy. Christians call this empowering factor the Holy Spirit.

Along with empowering the universe, this energy also animates and guides the formation of the human body. After conception, the energy releases with tremendous power, guiding the multiplication of a single cell into a human zygote. The zygote rapidly moves through all the evolutionary stages, resembling a fish, reptile, mammal, and primate before taking its final form as a human baby.

This rapid growth continues until early childhood. At that time, socialization begins, and the will is developed through potty training and behavior shaping. As the will grows stronger, you learn to constrain the energy to meet social necessities. First you gain control over the urge to urinate and defecate. Then you adjust your eating to meal times. Entering school, you learn to sit still and focus, rather than fidget or run around yelling and screaming like the free flowing energy might want you to do.

The sexual urge breaks out at puberty and this powerful force is similarly restrained to fit social patterns. The constraint of the energy is completed in your late teens and early twenties, as you become independent and take on all the tasks associated with supporting yourself in society. You may not notice it, but life tends to lose some of its glow and glory at this point. The nervous system stops evolving to a finer and finer state, and gradually the process of decay sets in.

Although captured and enslaved for social and survival purposes, the life energy is still there in adulthood. Athletes and dancers who engage in regular, vigorous exercise sometimes release the energy in unfettered movement. So do artists, writers, and scientists who engage in deep concentration for hours at a time and enjoy flashes of insight. Devotional types may feel their energy burst forth in heartfelt poetry and song.

For most of these people, the peak experience passes and the energy goes back to sleep. For a fortunate few, the energy release restarts their growth process, and they go on to develop remarkable degrees of power, genius, or saintliness.

Natural Meditation comes from a long lineage of teachers who learned how to liberate the life energy through surrendered action. It was developed by thousands of sincere meditators going down blind alleys and eventually finding their way to the highest states of consciousness and fulfillment in life.

Swami Kripalu was one of these experimenters, and he's provided us with a broad perspective on the spiritual growth process, based upon his lifetime of practice and scripture study. Through a proper understanding of the methods of Natural Meditation, you can release this energy and allow it to purify the body and mind, and galvanize your evolution.

When the disciples of Jesus received the Holy Spirit from heaven on the day of Pentecost, their purification began immediately, right there in the public square, as they talked in tongues, twisted and rolled about, and sang out to God. They eventually became outstanding saints, but at the outset they were quite ordinary people, just like you and me.

During my first visit to Swami Kripalu, I was going out the door after having said good-bye to him, when he called me and the translator back into the room. He wrote on his chalkboard, "The name of this yoga is love." I did not know what he meant at the time. Now I have a pretty good idea.

Sooner or later, we all close down energetically because the world hurts and takes advantage of us. We become hard-hearted. Surrender is a method of releasing our life energy that opens the heart.* So in the final analysis, love and surrender are really the same thing.

*Here's a summary of the surrender method presented so far:

(1) Let things be as they are, surrendering control of your body, mind, and feelings to an Absolute you trust completely.
(2) Let this Absolute or "the Divine hand" guide your meditation.
(3) Accept whatever happens as purification and grace.
(4) Surrender only to the Absolute.

Chapter Sixteen
A Natural Progression

While the surrender method is not scientific, Natural Meditation follows a predictable progression. Roughly the same things will happen to you that happen for everyone. This is not to say that individual differences and even an occasional miracle don't occur, because they do, but there's a basic pattern and the remedies for common problems apply in every case.

At the outset of practice, you'll experience a period of nothing happening. You've surrendered the will, but nothing has taken its place. This period may be a few seconds, a few hours, a few days, or even a few months. Not many people will continue meditating an hour or two a day for months without anything happening. This is the first barrier to get through, and if you stick with it something will eventually happen.

Usually something happens within a few minutes of surrendering. If you relinquish the will completely, the body may simply collapse on the floor.*   That is something. Eventually the life energy will begin to move the body into purifying actions and postures, whether or not you've ever heard of yoga.

*This is only one of many gateways to the realm of surrendered action. Swami Kripalu entered through the build up of life energy that occurred during his practice of pranayama and breath retention. Afterwards, he pointed to passionate orators unaware of their automatic gestures, artists so absorbed in their work that their actions became spontaneous, and even people moving unconsciously in deep sleep. In Kripalu Yoga practice, access can occur in the flow of relaxed and mindful movements, or the prolonged holding then release of willful postures.

This is likely to start in a rather sloppy fashion. Perhaps the legs reach out, but you can't touch your toes. Maybe you're stiff in the back, fat in the belly, and tense in the legs. If that's the case, you won't be able to do the forward bend properly in a hatha yoga sense.

In Natural Meditation, you will automatically adjust the posture based upon your body's needs. As it repeats again and again during meditation, you'll find yourself shifting from variation to variation, with the motion growing more precise over time. Eventually you'll end up in the classic yoga posture. The same thing happens with pranayama, as different breath patterns occur. The breath tends to start out ragged and shallow, growing refined and deep over time.

Kriyas and mudras will also occur. A kriya is a "purifying movement" that cleanses, heals, or strengthens the body in some way. A mudra is an "energy seal" that causes energy to build to high levels in a particular part of the body or nervous system. What begins as a floppy motion of the hands may evolve into a precise and potent yogic rite in its final expression.

In the earlier stages of practice, you are likely to go through active movements which vary considerably from one person to another. You may roll around on the floor, jump up and down swearing in Russian, or bang your head on the floor. After the energy has moved around a lot, it is likely to slow down to nothing. At this point, you may go into yogic sleep.

You may think that you should be alert and active, but sleep is coming naturally. If you have truly surrendered, you let sleep come. Whatever happens, let it happen! There is only one condition: you must surrender your body, mind and feelings to the Truth. If you've done that, there can be no error in your practice.*

As you keep surrendering, the life energy purifies and awakens the evolutionary force.** This core energy starts to rise and pierce the spinal centers in serial order. At this juncture, you will probably be doing the intermediate form of the postures with various pranayama and mudras.

It's significant that everyone eventually does the same postures, kriyas, and mudras. This shows that there's an inherent progression that comes from the physiology of the body. The energy is going somewhere. It's acting to evolve the body and mind in a definite direction.

Swami Kripalu was photographed demonstrating the final stages for a book called *Asana and Mudra*.*** When I saw those pictures, I thought to myself, "My body is never going to do those poses."

Then one day I was meditating, and the body just wanted to move into this position, then that position. I had been moving this way for fifteen or twenty minutes, feeling very calm and

*This guidance is meant to give a practitioner wide latitude to surrender and trust the rightness of whatever happens.

**Yoga distinguishes between prana, the life energy that runs and heals the body, and kundalini, which Swami Kripalu called the evolutionary force. Prana purifies the body and then awakens this stronger evolutionary force.

***The first section of *Asana and Mudra* can be downloaded at www.naturalmeditation.com.

blissful. Then I noticed my body was in an incredible posture, and I was paying no attention to it at all. This is Natural Meditation.

When the energy moves to the throat, a parallel process may happen with chanting. You may start with garbled English. That may lead you to dance around the room, chanting like a Jewish cantor, a Muslim calling worshipers to prayer, or a Native American medicine man.

Going from one sound pattern to the next, you might chant the basic sounds of all the languages. Your brain is being purified. After this, you may chant a final sound – OM – and then move into anahat nada, spontaneous singing from the heart as the emotions get purified too.

The mind goes through a similar purification process. At first, the mind is loaded with doubt. You'll wonder, "Am I making this happen? Is energy really moving? Is God doing this, or is it just my ego?" Everyone experiences this confusion to some degree. As the energy releases fully, the underlying doubt gets dispelled.

Then you're likely to find yourself having all these thoughts. "What's going to happen next? You know, I forgot to balance my checkbook. I don't think Suzy loves me anymore. Maybe I ought to stop having these thoughts?" You may get five or six of these trains of thought running simultaneously.

While it may seem intolerable, this is only mental purification, and it happens to everyone. Your mind will move from being dull, to being active and passionate, to being tranquil. It's a predictable sequence.

Along the way, surrender will clear your mind, digging out the deepest, darkest, most perverted desires that could ever exist. All your primitive fears and buried conflicts will also surface. Surrender is bringing this unconscious material into awareness to purify it away.

At some point, the mind goes through something that reminds me of scene from an old movie I saw once. A bunch of kids were sitting in this unhitched covered wagon. One of them accidentally released the brake, and the wagon started rolling down a hill. Some mothers noticed and began running after it. They weren't fast enough, so the men hopped on their horses and gave chase, but the wagon kept going faster and faster. Everybody was shouting, screaming and panicking. The action got louder and wilder. And then the wagon went off a cliff! As it flew through the air, there was a sudden silence.

A similar thing happens to the mind. It gets busier and busier. It reaches a frantic pitch. Finally it goes fffssssssst. Something dies at this point. Not you, but the agitated ego mind trying to keep itself safe and entertained.

Eventually the mind gets so pure it just goes to nothing. Your attention gets drawn deeply inside, away from the turmoil of the senses. You can still think, but you know they're just thoughts. Concentration, meditation and peace come naturally then.

There is only one thing left to do – keep surrendering. You may experience a pink dawn of love coming to you slowly and beautifully. You do not have to make this happen, or even evaluate the experience. Everything turns to love, and this is a love that stays.

At a certain point, samadhi or union begins. Samadhi is beyond the mind and senses. It's impossible to adequately describe. But it may be helpful to know that through samadhi you come to know directly that what you are, and what God is, are the same. Your own true, divine nature comes into union with God or Truth.

There are two stages of samadhi. The first is called sabija samadhi which means "with seed" equanimity. There is union, but seed desires and the reasoning power of the mind remain. The surrender process is not finished, and a depth process of self-inquiry will naturally occur in your meditation to take you beyond the mind.

When it came to surrendering my reason and judgment, I slammed my foot on the brakes to stop the process. I was attached to being able to discern what was really happening in life and afraid that I would lose this power. If I turned my judgment and reasoning faculties over to God, wouldn't I become an idiot? What would become of me if I let go of my ability to discriminate between right and wrong, left and right, and up and down? While it is true that there were some days when I could hardly speak, taking that step produced the greatest gain I'd made in meditation up to that point.

In the final stage of nirbija or "without seed" samadhi, the mind is dissolved away. Your mind becomes no-mind. You may think to yourself, "What will I do then?" You need not worry, for at this point you will truly be in God's hands.*

* In 2004, Yogeshwar summarized the stages of Natural Meditation as follows:

1. The body performs purifying actions.
2. The life energy is restrained and elevated.
3. The attention withdraws from the senses, the evolutionary force awakes, and the mind is purified.
4. You enter deep concentration.
5. You fall into spontaneous meditation.
6. You experience samadhi and Divine union.

Steps 1-3 correspond to Hatha Yoga. Steps 4-6 correspond to Raja Yoga.

How firmly or loosely a practitioner should hold any theoretical model of what will happen as a result of surrender is a question of debate. Swami Kripalu clearly believed there was an organic sequence that included a great number of postures, pranayamas, kriyas, and more importantly ten maha (great) mudras. He saw these mudras as the spine of kundalini yoga and essential energetic transformations necessary for a true samadhi.

In practice, considerable individual differences seem to exist, and some individuals practicing surrender meditation don't find themselves doing postures at all. Perhaps the integrating factor is to remember that the core practice is surrender to the Absolute, and not what takes place afterward.

Chapter Seventeen
How to Practice

Making the free choice to surrender to the way things truly are will transform your life. Resistance is the mechanism that causes you to accumulate physical tensions and mental impressions. Instead of resisting reality, choose to accept it. As resistance disappears, your body and mind will clear and the veil of delusion separating you from Truth will lift.

Everything that results from Natural Meditation is a side effect of this choice to surrender. This includes all the postures, energy seals, breathing patterns, and meditation experiences. Practice periods are formal times to say, "All right, I'll let things be," in a surrounding that lets your process unfold to great depths.

To begin practice, it's important to have a suitable space in which to meditate. A room ten feet by twelve feet is optimal, with a thick but firm pad in the middle where you sit and just let go. If you don't have enough space, you'll feel cramped and find yourself reining in actions that take you off your mat. Stopping anything that naturally wants to happen is a willful action, and this will keep your meditation shallow. You may or may not have an altar; that's up to you.

Swami Kripalu taught me to meditate in a locked room with the curtains drawn. Privacy is essential, as there is no way to go deeply into meditative states if you are afraid of someone walking in, or ridiculing you for wild actions or making noise. There is no way to reach the higher limits of this practice with other people around. Tell your family, friends or neighbors: "Don't pay any attention to the sounds. I'm just doing my yoga meditation."

Teachers often initiate groups into Natural Meditation, and some teachers of this technique have people meditate exclusively in groups. Group practice is okay for beginners, but after five to seven sessions individuals should meditate on their own. You don't have total freedom in a group format. Swami Kripalu taught me total freedom, and I advise you to practice alone.

It's best to meditate every day at the same time. Normally it is best to do your practice first thing in the morning. Get up an hour earlier; use the toilet; take a shower or bath; and have an empty stomach. If you sit down in your meditation spot at the same time each day, the routine becomes easy to maintain after a few weeks.

If possible, meditate for at least one hour. If you meditate less, you will not feel the full benefit of this technique. At the outset, don't go over or under that time allotment. As your practice progresses, speak to your teacher if you want to increase your meditation time. *

Begin your session with a prayer or affirmation. "God, I surrender this body, this mind, and these feelings to you." Express whatever is meaningful to you. Then sit straight, with your eyes closed, and start either ocean sounding or alternate nostril breathing. Continue breathing until the energy starts to move, or the body gets tired. At that point, completely let go of your willful control. Allow the mind, body, and feelings to do what they do – or do not do – as guided by the Divine hand.

*Swami Kripalu taught that householders could engage in spiritual practices for up to two hours per day. Increasing practice beyond that level puts a practitioner at risk of becoming disenchanted with his or her professional duties and family responsibilities.

Once you have let go of control, do not engage in willful actions during meditation. If you ignore this instruction, your doubt about the life energy will not resolve. It is better to lie there without a finger moving hour after hour than it is to act willfully.

If you don't do this, every time the energy starts to move you will think, "There is no life energy here; this is a bunch of hogwash. I just wanted to move, so I moved." This doubt is likely to cause you to cease practicing. My instruction to you is to surrender completely, neither doing willful actions, nor willfully preventing anything that wants to happen from happening through to completion.

In willful meditation, you either concentrate on some focal point, or willfully try to maintain a state of openness. In Natural Meditation, you surrender control to the Absolute and trust the life energy to guide the attention in the way needed to make the most rapid progress in your meditation. Do not try to focus your mind on any particular thing. Let the attention go wherever it wants.

After the pre-determined time for meditation has passed, end with a prayer of thanks. Take a few minutes to return to normal consciousness, and leave the room.

Meditation should continue for the allotted time and not be cut short because you get distracted. If you find yourself thinking, "Well, it feels like my practice is over and it's time to end," don't believe it. You will go through varying levels of contact with the environment in Natural Meditation. If you stay with the practice, you will discover that you are not really coming out of meditation. You are just changing from one state to another.

It helps to keep your eyes closed, willfully if necessary, for your first six months of meditation. After that, introversion will be established and you can let your eyes do what they want.

Your meditation experience may not always be what you want. Sometimes meditation is boring. You may find your mind doing seemingly pointless things, like formulating the grocery list. Perhaps that's what needs to be done. The life energy is trying to release your attention from the grocery list so it can move on to other things.

If you say to yourself, "Oh, I shouldn't be thinking about the grocery list; so I'm not going to think about it; I am going to think about God," you are using your will. It's all well and good to think about God, but you are going against the method that will bring you in union with God. If you surrender, the life energy will guide the attention appropriately.

You should give this practice a trial period of at least three weeks. Do it every day for an hour and see what happens. If at the end of three weeks you have not gotten some positive results or encouragement, you may choose not to go on.

If you do find success with this technique, resist the urge to proselytize that often afflicts neophytes. If people are naturally drawn to this practice, let them come. If they ask questions, answer them honestly and direct them to an experienced teacher, but be aware that this practice is not for everyone.

If you take up Natural Meditation seriously, your system will be purified. In the process, you will go through periods of mental, emotional and physical disturbance. You may break out in a rash, or have intestinal disturbances, diarrhea or cramps. You may feel weepy and want to cry for no apparent reason. You may seem to go temporarily crazy.

These healing crises may last for a day, or two, or three. Do not panic, as this is part of the purification process. There is no smooth way to a healthy physical, emotional, and mental state because true healing always involves a healing crisis. Just keep on with your meditation, and in a few days all your symptoms will be gone.

For those doing more hours of meditation, the purification may be more intense or last longer. You will probably think that you are ill, and you may indeed be ill, as old diseases are brought to the surface and their symptoms recur. If you want to consult a medical practitioner, do so. The mistake at this point is to stop your daily practice. If you keep doing your meditation and surrender completely, things should straighten out in three to six days.

Pay attention if you get really irritable, mentally unstable, intolerant or paranoid. This is a sign your energy may be flowing upward and carrying impurities into the brain. Cut back on your meditation time, as you are probably overdoing it, and seek appropriate guidance.

People following the teachings of Natural Meditation in the tradition of my teacher meditate from one to eight hours a day in a locked room so they do not have to worry about the world. When they come out of meditation, they reengage their will, treat others well, and behave ethically. Practicing this way, surrender eventually pervades their lives.

I am not trying to sell you on surrender. You have the power of choice, and I do not expect everyone who hears this message to follow it. You can choose how you want to be with the Truth of life. Your basic options are to fight, play, or surrender.

It's my job to tell you about surrender and make it clear that the doorway is open to you. If you walk through and ask questions, I will do my very best to guide you. I just point to the door. That's my duty.

Chapter Eighteen
Who Should Practice?

If you choose to practice Natural Mediation, your progress may be fast or slow. The rate of your progress will depend on the depth of your surrender, how much time you spend in meditation, the previous work you've done in this and other lifetimes, and the quality of your spiritual teacher.

Because Natural Meditation is not for everyone, I developed the following requirements to determine whether to initiate an aspirant into the practice.*

My first requirement is that you must want to grow, evolve, get closer to God, or personally experience the Absolute Truth, and you must want to pursue these goals through the process of surrender.

My second requirement is that you want to experience this Absolute Truth more than you want success, accomplishment, wealth, and status. I am not talking about renouncing the world, joining a religious order, or putting on robes. Those are surface things.

I am talking about whether you have the honest, heartfelt intention to put the Truth first. To practice surrender, you must be willing to allow your attachments, desires, and personal goals to be dissolved away and replaced by the desirelessness of union with God.

*Yogeshwar taught Natural Meditation within the guru/disciple relationship central to traditional yoga.

Swami Kripalu believed that people are of different natures. Some are action-oriented, others are intellectually-oriented, and still others are heart-oriented. My third requirement is that you have already developed your nature to an exceptional level. If you do not display a high degree of skillfulness, intelligence, or devotion, you should stay with willful practices until you have done so.

My fourth requirement applies only to married people, whom I will not initiate without the permission of their spouse. The spouse does not necessarily have to do Natural Meditation, but he or she has to understand that their spouse may lose his or her ambition, goals, and drive toward success in life. Since the purpose of Natural Meditation and the marriage may come into conflict in the future, I require this at the outset.

My last requirement is that I will not initiate anyone with whom I do not feel a positive connection. A teacher must know that a student will at least try to follow his guidance. Unless I am confident of that, I will not go forward.

When I give initiation, a spark of life energy or drop of pure Divine Love is given to each person.* I watch the group, and each one surrenders. Many can only sustain their surrender for about a tenth of a second. Something starts to happen. A rush

---

* Yogeshwar's students commenced their practice after an initiation ritual called *shaktipat diksha*, literally *descent of the power*. Traditionally described as a transference of spiritual energy from an awakened guru that quickens the life force of a fit disciple, it is not clear whether the ritual was simply permission to surrender deeply and allow energy to move. Regardless, it was effective at bringing forth surrendered action. Perhaps more importantly, it established a clear bond between teacher and student supportive of ongoing guidance.

of energy comes through the body, a movement starts to happen, or something explodes in the mind. Instantly they grab back on with their will to reassert their patterned personality because they are terrified of the unknown.

If this is the case for you, face it. You can only start from where you are. So you have the capacity to surrender for a tenth of a second. What would it look like to really do that? "Okay, I surrender. Whoops, I don't know if I like this surrender business or not. I'll surrender my feelings. Hmm, that caused me to pull back. This time I'll try surrendering my thoughts." Eventually you'll find something you can surrender a little bit for a little while, and your growth will begin.

People often say to me, "I want to surrender, but I don't know how." This is not true. Surrender is not a matter of knowing how; it's a question of how courageous and determined you are. You can surrender anytime, any place, under any circumstances.

The real question is whether you can stand the reaction to having surrendered. Surrender is a profound choice. It's heavy; that's its nature. If you make the choice to surrender control, the Truth comes knocking whether you like it or not, and purification starts to occur spontaneously.

It's fairly common for a person seeking initiation to say something like, "Everyone is doing this technique; maybe it can help me get over my asthma." Natural Meditation is not a method for people wanting help with their problems. I direct people like this to other techniques likely to improve their health.

While less common, people also ask to be initiated because they've heard that awakening the evolutionary force will give them more creative power to fulfill their desires. That's not the purpose of Natural Meditation either. Natural Meditation is for individuals wanting to grow and evolve toward the Absolute Truth, God, and Divine Love through the process of surrender.

One of my students came to me recently. She had made real progress, and I was surprised when she said, "I'm thinking about quitting this meditation."

I asked, "What's happened?" She answered, "If I keep going, I'm going to become a saint." She had an intuitive sense of where she was headed and honestly didn't know if she could deal with having her heart opened to the extent of feeling love for everyone.

How far you progress in Natural Meditation depends upon your ability to get through crises like that. They come up, and if you stick with your practice they get resolved by some mysterious grace. All that's in your hands is the choice to surrender or fight the process.

Chapter Nineteen
Ten Feet by Ten Feet

After I had spent some months with Swami Kripalu in India, I went to our final meeting and asked: "Is there anything else I need to know before I leave?"

At this point, I had not asked a question for three weeks, but I asked this one just in case I had missed something.

He said, "No, there is nothing, only this," and told me the following story.

"Once there was a true seeker on a long journey. Night fell and he lost his way in the darkness. In his despair, he saw a light glowing in the distance. Making his way to the light, he knocked on the door of a hut he found there.

A holy man came to the door and said, 'What is it, my son?'

'I've lost my way,' said the seeker, 'can you help me?'

'I cannot go with you,' said the holy man, 'but I will give you my lantern.' Then he gave the seeker a lantern.

The seeker held up the lantern and said, 'But I cannot find my way with this lantern. On this dark night, I can only see ten feet and I have many miles to travel before morning.'

The holy man replied, 'That's true, but if you walk ten feet, you will see another ten feet clearly. When you have gone that far, you will see another ten feet illumined. So ten feet by ten feet, you will find your way.' Then the holy man closed the door."

After relating that story, Swami Kripalu explained that this technique of Natural Meditation was my lantern. As long as I kept doing it, I would find my way. And I have found this to be correct. I have given you here what you need to know. The rest is up to you. You do not need to have constant contact with a teacher. Keep at it, and you will find your way.

Only three things will give you trouble: the creative plexus, sustaining plexus, and dissolving plexus.* To get through these three knots, you need the assistance of an experienced teacher, scripture, or God. Otherwise, just keep doing your practice.

I recommend that you follow the path of moderation. Do your work, get your education, get married, own a home if you like, and have a family. Stay in the world, but be not of the world. To do this, limit your possessions, eat moderately, be good and kind to people, and moderate your meditation by agreement with your spouse.

If a time comes when you feel that you have had enough of worldly life, if you grow tired of the endless cycle of having and fulfilling desires, then you can adopt the path of renouncing all desires. But do not be premature in this. Let it come by God's hand.**

*These are the three granthis known in hatha yoga as bio-energetic constrictions that block the ascent of the life force. The brahma-granthi is made up of the first three energy centers and located in the belly region. The vishnu-granthi is at the throat, and the rudra-granthi is at the brow. These knots must be undone by the life force so energy can flow freely and ascend.

**This chapter ends part two of the book on Natural Meditation. The remaining chapters come from talks delivered later in Yogeshwar's life and selected to summarize his teachings.

Chapter 20
Beyond All Viewpoints

This is the last formal talk that I will give in public, and you will be the last people to be burdened by my technicality and heaviness. Hereafter, we'll just gather to have a good time.*

Maybe you came here to be entertained, but I'm not going to entertain you. I am going to lay the Truth on you, and I am going to lay it on heavy. Then I am going to quit. You'll probably all quit after this talk too!

I'm going to talk about viewpoint and identification. You wouldn't think these were very important subjects, but they make the difference between leading an ordinary life and leading a successful, spiritual life.

It's not difficult to understand viewpoint. There is the visual and auditory viewpoint, like the one from which you are seeing and hearing me now. At the center of all your senses is a perceptual viewpoint; that's one type of viewpoint.

Another type of viewpoint is emotional, like "Oh God, when is this talk going to end?" or "This is too much for me to take in and deal with." There are also attitudinal viewpoints, like "I'm no good," or "I'm glorious," or "I hate everyone, especially myself."

We become identified with these perceptual, emotional, and mental viewpoints, and they color every experience of our whole life. There is really nothing wrong with these viewpoints

*Excerpted from a talk given to close students in Flaxley, South Australia on an unknown date.

and attitudes, and there's not even anything wrong with being identified with them. They arise naturally through the process of living. The problem is being stuck in them.

Even the attitude "everyone hates me" won't be a problem if you can drop it to pick up the attitude "everyone loves me" when circumstances change. But if you're stuck in the "everyone hates me" attitude, someone can come into your life who really does love you, who tries to pour out his or her heart to you, but your response will be, "No, you're just saying that. You're pretending." If you are really stuck in this attitude, you will end up with zero love in your life.

The answer is not to swing like a pendulum to the other side. If you get stuck in the attitude "everyone loves me," you will not be able to participate in reality. You have one viewpoint, and in practice it is not true. Everybody does not love you. With this attitude, you won't be able to see how things truly are. Attitudes are fine. Identification is fine. Going into them and going out of them is fine. Being stuck is the problem.

You would think that a discussion like this would set you free, but we're a lot more stuck and fixated than you might imagine. A large portion of the yogic life is gaining independence from these habitual emotional and attitudinal viewpoints.* First you get unstuck, and then you go beyond all viewpoints. But you've got to get unstuck first.

It's when we resist the way things truly are that our spiritual connection to the Absolute is severed, and we take the viewpoint that we are just a human being, a body lost in the apparent illusion of life. We are so emotionally committed, so

*In addition to Holistic Yoga (see page 68) Yogeshwar developed and taught a sophisticated curriculum of mind clearing techniques.

stuck, and so fixated in this human viewpoint that we cannot seriously entertain anything else. We see ourselves as things, a physical object existing in time and space.

Absolute Truth does not manifest itself. It's the potential behind everything. Metaphysically speaking, all that really exists is the true individual that you are, the Divine Other, and the connection between these two. That connection is the central energy channel of the body, the sushumna nadi. You are at one end, and God is at the other. I warned you that I was going to get heavy.

Practitioners of yoga adopt one of two basic viewpoints. The first is the viewpoint of will, and the second is the viewpoint of surrender. It's not that one is right and the other is wrong, or that one is higher and the other lower. Each is a valid viewpoint on a central Truth, and together they give rise to two different paths. Willful yoga is effective at purifying you. Surrender yoga evolves you. These are two tasks of any aspirant on the path of yoga: purification and evolution.

Anything that helps you to stop resisting and going against the way things truly are will align and purify you. When enough purification has happened, the connection between you and Divine Otherness will be a straight line and evolution will start to take place.

I've experienced this in meditation. When energy flow is limited to the lower centers, your attention is externalized. The eyes, nose, ears, tongue, and sense of touch give rise to a perceptual viewpoint, and you are identified with your body.

At the brow center is the mind and all the mental and emotional viewpoints that form the basis of our personality. When you're identified here, you take the human viewpoint we are all familiar with.

Slightly above that is no viewpoint at all. I don't mean an absence of interchange, or a temporarily stopped flow of consciousness. That would be an unconscious state of trance or swoon. I mean the senses and mind have been transcended. You are conscious with no viewpoint, but there is still a subtle identification as total openness.

Above the brow center is samadhi, the union between you and Divine Otherness. There is still no viewpoint, but now with no identification and total consciousness. This is your only true identity; anything else is identification with some relative viewpoint.

When your energy reaches these higher levels, reality looks different. When there is no residue remaining from the past, when there are no delusions that you are laboring under, there is no difference between you and the Truth. Union at last has happened.

Chapter 21
The Road to Liberation

I am no longer a teacher. I spent fifty-five years teaching. Now I am retired and spend my time meditating and writing. However, I am here visiting two good friends, who are also your teachers, and they have asked me say a few words.*

You are householders; you have families; and therefore you must be actively engaged in earning a living. With all these responsibilities, why should I talk to you about liberation?

No matter how successful, your life must be aimed at liberation to have meaning. By all means enjoy happiness, health, family, pleasure, and make lots of money. But if you are not progressing along the road to liberation as you do these things, you will find yourself going in circles. You will turn fifty and say, "What was that about? My family is grown. I have enough money to live. What is the meaning of it all? Why am I alive?" This is what happens when you put survival first, and the road to liberation second.

How do you get on the road? The first step is to realize who you are. Most of us are confused at this fundamental level. We see ourselves as a name, or the activity we do in life: "I'm John, the electrician." We only have superficial knowledge of ourselves, and we don't get anything out of the lives we are leading as a result. You start on the road by directly experiencing yourself as you truly are. It's simple – "I'm me" – and it comes from directly experiencing the one you are.

The next step is to realize what you are. If you directly experience who you are even a little bit, you will immediately

*Excerpted from four talks given near Udine, Italy, in August 1998.

begin asking, "What is it that I am? Am I a body? A brain? A personality? A soul? What am I?" As you work on that question, layer after layer of false identification falls away.

I can tell you what you are right now, but it won't give you the direct experience you need to shift the trajectory of your life. You are not a physical entity that can die or be destroyed. You are not a victim of life that must act against his or her will in order to survive. That's the illusion of this world. You are a divine individual who has the power of choice. And at the same time, you have a body that can die.

Enlightenment Intensives are specifically designed to enable participants to realize who and what they are. There are other ways to do this, but this is one way.

The next step is success in life. Yes, success is on the road to liberation. Once you have correct knowledge that you are a divine individual instead of a physical body, you will discover there's a power in that. You can originate your whole life from the direct knowledge of who and what you are. To do that, you will need to develop your communication skills, powers of concentration, and something I call energy mastery. All of these skills can be easily learned through willful techniques if you know who and what you are.

Each of us has creative energy arising within us, and if it's channeled correctly it will empower you and lead to success. There are two secrets to energy mastery. The first is that you have to put a limit on your sexual expression. If all your energy is consumed in sexual activity, there's nothing left over to direct into other pursuits.

The second secret is that you won't let your energy grow strong if you are likely to hurt others. You must commit to behaving ethically and treating others well before you will release your life energy and let it rise up. If you feel you've mistreated others, this can be a block.

Everyone makes mistakes. Some are big, and some are little, but everybody makes them. I can attest to that, having made a number of gigantic mistakes. Sometimes I look back and it seems like a cartoon. You don't have to redo your wrong choices. Just commit to following dharma – be kind, be truthful, exercise restraint, and respect others. That commitment is sufficient.

If you follow these steps, you will attain some level of success in life and naturally get to the point where your only desire is for liberation. When you've applied yourself to life's challenges, when you've become an accomplished person, and when your children are grown, what are you going to do? You can only take so many trips. You can only watch so much television. You are likely to find at this point that you don't want excitement or pleasure, you want a truer and deeper level of fulfillment. You want to be free, and the way to that is to stop denying others and resisting the way things are.

If you get to this point, you will want to know what to do next, so listen closely. There are many ways to approach the road to liberation, and they are all equally valuable. All the approaches, however, eventually converge on a single road. You must surrender; you must give over control to the Ultimate; and you must find a way to release your life energy.

The road is well known and well marked. My teacher called it Sahaja Yoga, and I have called it Natural Meditation. My advice to you is to find an experienced teacher. Strictly speaking, a teacher is not necessary. But it is a long journey and there are so many pitfalls on the way that you will need a teacher to pull you out of the pit, brush you off, and say "Go on again." Otherwise you will do the practice, and all the right things will happen, but you will misinterpret them and give up. That's why you should take up Natural Meditation only if you are ready to give your whole life to the endeavor.

What's it like to be liberated? A liberated person lives in the truth of what they are, and what others are. A liberated person is happy and is not pushed around by life. A liberated person enjoys himself, but he is not seeking to enjoy life. It doesn't matter so much what is happening to him. Whatever it is, he can enjoy it. This only comes from being purified and evolved through surrender, energy awakening, and hatha and raja yoga.

Perhaps you are only going to work on your personal growth and success this time around. That's fine, so start on the road by discovering for yourself who and what you are. Learn to concentrate and channel your energy. Become a powerful and a kind person. In this way you will not only be very successful, but you will be growing and preparing for liberation.

I believe that it's important to know about the road to liberation even if you are not going to take up Natural Meditation in this lifetime. It puts all the survival tasks of your life into a bigger context. It makes you aware of the importance of treating others well, and as long as you are moving down the road you will not feel like you are going round and round in circles.

You have the power to do whatever you want in life. Yes, it may take a long time. Yes, it may take a great commitment and a lot of effort, practice and study. If liberation was easy, we would all have been liberated long ago. Whether you choose to go on this road or not, my love for you is the same. Even if nothing else, we have had this contact. I love you all. Ciao.

Afterword

Readers should know that the bulk of this book is representative of Yogeshwar Muni's teachings during the 1970s and 1980s. He continued to practice and teach for another quarter century until his death in 2007.

During those years, Yogeshwar developed a body of metaphysical teachings called the *Lila Paradigm* through which he tried to shed light on the nature of consciousness and provide a basis for the unification of science and religion. Readers who wish to continue their study of Truth contemplation are directed to this resource.

Yogeshwar also carefully rendered an English edition of Swami Kripalu's commentary on the Hatha Yoga Pradipika entitled *Revealing the Secret* which was published in 2002. Readers wanting to continue their study of Natural Meditation are directed to this scriptural text.

Late in his life, Yogeshwar reviewed and updated the Enlightenment Intensive teaching manuals that serve as the basis for the first half of this book. After completing that task in 2006, he wrote: "There is nothing I have found in all my spiritual experiences, including the depths of samadhi, that in any way contradicts the Enlightenment Intensive. In fact, it has done nothing but validate and reinforce it."

A library of Yogeshwar's teachings, including the works cited above, can be found online at www.naturalmeditation.net. Thank you for your interest in this book. May you be guided and protected in your practice.

Appendix
The Two Paths
Discourse by Swami Kripalu

Editor's Introduction

On January 14, 1978, Yogeshwar Muni and his ashram community gathered in St. Helena, California, to commemorate Swami Kripalu's 65th birthday. Swami Kripalu delivered the following talk, which has been excerpted to focus on the topics explored in this book. Serious students will wish to study the complete transcript available at www.naturalmeditation.net.

Discourse Opening

Lovers of God, lovers of guru, spiritual brothers and sisters, and everyone. Over and over, may God be glorified. My love to you!

Today you have gathered here for my birthday celebration. I am a swami who has renounced the world to free myself from the bondage of birth and death. If birth is bondage, then what is the importance of a birthday celebration? None! However this is my viewpoint, and not yours. You are celebrating, and I am your invited, loving guest.

There are two aspects of any celebration. The external aspect is food. The internal aspect is the study of spiritual principles. Now I will give you an introduction to the two paths of yoga.

The path of will makes use of the mind and its impressions. It is meant for those engaged in an active life in the world. The path of will builds character and brings its practitioner success in life.

The path of surrender dissolves the impressions in the mind. It is meant for those who have abandoned worldly activities and want only the Absolute. Spiritual aspirants should understand both paths perfectly.

The Path of Will

When human beings were first born on the earth, life was extremely difficult. For eons, humanity struggled just to survive. Individuals raised without good character become wanton, and humanity suffered from their unethical actions.

Eventually humankind was able to establish a virtuous system of life called dharma to foster happiness and peace. Love, cooperation, self-control, and service to family, and society are the foremost aspects of dharma. These guiding principles counter our tendency toward hatred, selfishness, and tyranny.

Dharma appears to be ordinary. If it were ordinary, it would have been practiced from the beginning. The fact that dharma took many centuries to be established proves that it is extraordinary.

In order to practice dharma and enjoy its benefits, those living in society must learn techniques for controlling their sexual energy and mind. This is the essence of the willful spiritual path. When the energy and mind are tranquil, good health, virtuous actions, and success result. When the energy and mind are disturbed, it causes disease, distorted actions, and death.

First, we must instill love and tolerance into our own family. A smiling face, loving sweet speech, and treating everyone with respect are the keys to success. However one must be a yogi and not an actor.

A true yogi can also maintain self-control in the midst of society, where many disturbances are encountered. A task of this nature can be accomplished only through self-discipline and the help of a code of ethical precepts.

In the yogic scriptures, the importance of observing such restraints and observances is greatly stressed.* Everyone's mind is disturbed by acts of violence, lying, theft, adultery and avarice. Thus they are to be avoided, and the practice of non-violence, truthfulness, non-theft, chastity, charity, and many other positive qualities is recommended.

When one conforms his behavior to a code of ethical precepts, he is following a willful path. This code of restraints and observances is a glorious part of the yoga tradition, and there is a marvelous strength in it. Every outstanding person in any field is using some facet of these ethical principles to develop their character, be skillful in their actions, and succeed in life.

Skillfulness is not easily obtained and comes only through a sustained effort. An aspirant of willful dharma must keep constant control over his mind, remaining aware and permitting no disturbances to arise. Through ethical precepts and the other techniques of willful yoga, one gradually achieves mental control over the senses and organs of action.

Healthy diet and sexual restraint are the body of willful yoga. Aspirants must eat moderately. Those who are single should practice celibacy. Married householders should limit their sexual expression. Sexual energy should be directed into spiritual practice and fulfilling one's duties in life.

*This is a reference to yama and niyama, the restraints and observances often called the "ten commandments of yoga."

112

Yoga postures, pranayama, and meditation techniques are included in willful yoga. Postures are done in the correct sequence, passing from one to another slowly and smoothly, with ease and control of one's breath. Meditation techniques are used to steady the mind and gain control over the senses. and organs of action.

By doing these and other willful techniques, one develops good character and the following worldly powers: personal strength, determination, clear and logical thinking, good memory, creativity, and decisiveness. By directing the life energy with the mind, one can act skillfully and ethically to fulfill his or her desires and achieve wealth, pleasure, status, and true virtue.

In both willful yoga and surrender yoga, it is necessary to awaken the evolutionary force. Without this, it is not possible to grow spiritually. In willful yoga, the techniques of yoga are used to awaken the evolutionary force in its partial and tolerable form. This is the way for aspirants to spiritually develop while living a family life in society.

The Path of Surrender

The yoga of surrender is called by many names including natural yoga, siddha yoga, kriya yoga, and kundalini yoga. Surrender yoga is the path for outstanding individuals seeking only liberation. All yoga is included in it.

Mind is the source of bondage. Life energy is the source of liberation.* Because of this, a seeker of liberation avoids

*Mind is the source of bondage, because all mental models, concepts and subtle impressions obscure the Absolute Truth. The path to liberation is to awaken the life energy and pass through the rigors of the transformative process required to dissolve the mind.

willfully controlling his mind and lets the life energy flow naturally. Surrender yoga is unique in that the evolutionary force is awakened in its complete, uncontrollable, and terrifying form.

In willful yoga, the willpower is strengthened and becomes very powerful. The partially awakened life energy remains subject to the control of the mind. Thus the mind remains tranquil all day.

In surrender yoga, the released life energy is given total freedom and allowed to surge powerfully through the system. Total celibacy is practiced. As a result, the mind becomes unstable. Self-control can be lost at any time in response to an unexpected stimulation. Because of this instability, a surrender yogi must stay secluded in order to keep his life peaceful.

After the release of the life energy, a practitioner of surrender yoga has many meditation experiences and his enthusiasm greatly increases. However, he soon finds himself continually confronted by new challenges. To continue to progress, the study of scripture and guidance of a master teacher is essential. If faith is lost, the surrender yogi may become diseased, mad, or proceed down the wrong path.

When initiation into surrender yoga is given to weak-minded people, they are greatly harassed by the movement of life energy. They try to stop its flow, but they can't regain mental control.

Where willful yoga produces fit disciples, the path of surrender yoga produces great masters. Unless an aspirant succeeds at willful yoga, embarking on the path of surrender is like trying to jump from the earth to reach the feet of Almighty God. Only through willful yoga does an aspirant come to qualify for the path of surrender.

I was the only disciple to whom my guru gave initiation. At the time, I could not fathom why he was not initiating others. Now, through my own experience, I have come to understand. I believe a master yogi should give surrender initiation to four or five highly-qualified disciples who surrender completely and practice only yoga for the rest of their lives.

Closing

I did not plan to come to America, but God ordered me unexpectedly, and so I came at once. When I decided to make the long trip, Amrit Desai and Yogeshwar Muni were with me in India. Now I am here with them and you.

Each and every word of this discourse is filled with the experience of my yoga sadhana and scripture study. If you read it and reflect on it frequently, you will get new insights and realizations, as teachings are understood differently in different stages of practice.

I am at a stage in my yoga sadhana where I cannot plan even a short trip. Moreover, I cannot participate in any public activities. Yet today I have done so because of your love. By the grace of Almighty, Merciful God, I have not experienced any difficulty. Instead, I have accepted your love and respectful prostrations with pleasure. I give you my blessings.

May everyone be happy. May everyone be healthy. May everyone be prosperous. May no one be unhappy.

Your loving grandfather, Kripalu.

Editor's Commentary

Swami Kripalu subscribed to the traditional yogic view that the body's surplus energy and resources are used to produce sexual fluids. These fluids can either be dissipated in pleasure seeking (bhoga) or transmuted into nervous system development and spiritual growth (yoga).

A wholesome lifestyle coupled with self-restraint serves to uplift health and maximize the production of sexual fluids. For many practitioners, this results in a strong sex drive. Swami Kripalu taught that married householders should practice celibacy "to the best of their ability" with the ideal being "sexual relations once a month for the purposes of procreation." Excess sexual energy was to be sublimated into willful spiritual practices, an ethical livelihood viewed as service to society, and other positive life activities.

In the traditional yogic model, surrender yogis practice total celibacy. Without the outlet of marriage and life activities, sexual energy often torments these yogis in their spiritual practice. The challenge facing a surrender yogi is to find a way to reabsorb the sexual fluids into their blood stream, and raise the energy from the lower to the higher energy centers. This is the supposed source of a great yogi's power, radiance, and high consciousness.

Under this yogic view, spiritual growth is not possible without sexual restraint. Like steam generated by the boiling water of a steam engine, sexual fluids and libido are the unseen forces that make evolution possible.

Despite having studied modern physiology and the work of psychologists including Freud, Swami Kripalu was forthright

116

and unapologetic in teaching the pivotal role played by celibacy in yoga. For example, after clearly stating the "once a month for the purposes of procreation" guideline for householders, he went on to say in this talk, "No self-controlled householder should be dissatisfied with this noble limit, and it may be that any dissatisfied householder is not ready for the spiritual path."

Yogeshwar Muni and Amrit Desai modified Swami Kripalu's teaching on celibacy. Yogeshwar taught that householders should be "moderate in their sexual expression." In Amrit Desai's ashram, married couples were encouraged to live the yogic lifestyle and "be conscious and natural" in their sexual expression.

Ode to a Silent God

I would like you to speak,
but you adorn the morning
with your silence. One by
one, I place my doubts at
your feet where they seem
to disappear. "At your feet,"
is just a figure of speech.
I cannot picture you
in a body. In fact, I have
no name for you, though I've
tried hard to find one.
I surrender body, mind,
and heart, and then I give
my needs into the open space
of your incorporeal embrace.
Whatever I give you ceases
to be mine, and this is,
I think, a priceless gift.

I'd like to paint your portrait,
but within the ornate frame
there would be nothing but
light, and sometimes not
even that. A frame is too
confining, of course. Imagine
All That Is squeezed inside
four slim pieces of wood.

When I offer you my fear,
it is no longer here, but lifted
like a great weight off my chest.
Anxiety rises like a wave that
threatens to break me in a
million little pieces. I sit
with it, and something in me
witnesses without being sucked
into anxiety's warped reality.
Eventually I remember to
give you this distress, which
noticeably lessens, but still
nibbles at the edges of my psyche.

I feel so vulnerable,
so out of control, but also
washed clean and thoroughly
seen, as if I am entirely transparent.
I'd still like you to speak, but the
silence is so natural and easy.
Now that my breath and yours
are indistinguishable, words
might be intrusive. So I bow
to you in gratitude, and give
you my practice of surrender,
to do with what you will.

Danna Faulds

About the Editor

A chance 1981 encounter with Swami Kripalu shifted the trajectory of Richard Faulds' life. Already a student of yoga, he embarked on a daily practice of yoga, pranayama, and meditation, and forged a close affiliation with Kripalu Center that continues today. As a Kripalu Center staff member, Richard has worn many hats: volunteer, ashram resident, legal counsel, president, and senior teacher. Richard currently chairs Kripalu's Board of Trustees, and is best known in Kripalu circles by his Sanskrit name "Shobhan."

One of Richard's joys and missions in life is to practice the teachings of the Kripalu tradition and share them with others in contemporary terms. To serve that purpose, he earned a masters degree in Counseling and Human Development in 1996 which helped him integrate the views of East and West.

Richard has written *Kripalu Yoga: A Guide to Practice On and Off the Mat,* a comprehensive but easy-to-read book synthesizing the experience of the Kripalu community. He has also written two companion books to this volume titled *Sayings of Swami Kripalu: Inspiring Quotes from a Contemporary Yoga Master,* and *Swimming With Krishna: Teaching Stories from the Kripalu Yoga Tradition*, along with numerous articles for Kripalu Center publications, many of which can be found on the KYTA page of Kripalu's website.

Richard lives in the Shenandoah Valley of Virginia with his wife, poet Danna Faulds, where they practice yoga, tend a vegetable garden, and teach individuals and small groups interested in the Kripalu tradition. You can contact them by e-mail at yogapoems@aol.com.